Star Sign
Pisces

– Love, Relationhips, Work –

© Naumann & Göbel Verlagsgesellschaft mbH
Part of the VEMAG Verlags- und Medien Aktiengesellschaft, Cologne
Author: Alfred P. Zeller
Translator: Johanna Ellsworth
All rights reserved
ISBN 3-625-10491-1

Preface

This book is intended to provide you with a basic introduction to astrology. It will tell you a lot of things about yourself, some of which you may probably already know or have at least suspected, yet there will be so much more that is totally new and will surprisingly reveal abilities and strengths that you never knew you had. These will open up previously unthought of possibilities for a more satisfying and successful life. But you will also learn about your flaws and weaknesses, which are just as important: Only once you have recognised your own mistakes can you actively confront them and ensure that your life with others is more trouble-free and altogether happier.

Astrology is neither a kind of secret science shrouded in mystery nor is it a dubious way of predicting the future, and it is certainly not a comfortable excuse to renounce all personal responsibility on the grounds that your future is 'in the hands of the stars'. Instead it is mankind's oldest empirical science, founded on thousands of years of observation of the interplay of cosmic and earthly occurrences. Throughout the centuries the greatest minds of the day have dedicated themselves to its study: from the second century AD with the universal scholar Ptolemy to the dawning of the new age with the great physician and alchemist Paracelsus, the humanist Melanchthon and the founders of modern astronomy and the natural sciences: Copernicus, Galileo and Kepler. Even Goethe showed a keen interest in astrology, as can be seen from his works. Astrology starts from the premise that we are not isolated beings cut off from our surroundings, but are, moreover, embedded in a social, geographical and cosmic system, in a network of subtle correlations which both define and influence us. Cosmic 'clocks' regulate all living processes on earth and cosmic events bring about the change between day and night, and the changing of the seasons and of the tides. In fact, everything that happens on earth is defined and regulated either as a whole or individually by the cosmos. We have only recently found out – or to be more specific only recently re-discovered – the importance of the energy that is transmitted to us across the universe; re-discovered, since our predecessors suspected as much thousands of years ago.

However, it is not an empty shell that is defined by the cosmos but an individual living thing which has inherited genetically configured characteristics from its parents. How these genetically and cosmically defined innate abilities are realised depends on the surroundings in which the life unfolds. For this reason a horoscope alone cannot fully capture the multifariousness of a person and explain their life.

Serious astrology always takes the social surroundings of the person whose horoscope is being read into account. Astrology does not map out inevitabilities, for it is not intended to and cannot release the individual from or constrain them to any decisions. Instead it aims to counsel the individual to the right decision by helping to show their possibilities and limitations.

This book will therefore make it possible for you to discover which of your traits and abilities you have been given by the cosmos and will reveal to you your strengths and areas for possible development as well as your weaknesses and instabilities. The first half of the book will look at the two most important aspects of your own horoscope: your sun sign and your ascendant. These will be enriched by looking at Chinese and Native American astrology as well as the Celtic (Tree) Horoscope.

Your sun sign is the constellation in which the sun was on the day you were born; it is the most important cosmic defining feature. Since time immemorial each sign of the zodiac has been divided into three decades in order to achieve a more specific degree of differentiation: in the first decade there is a residual influence of the previous sign of the zodiac, whereas in the third decade there is an increased influence of the subsequent sign, in the second decade, however, neither of the neighbouring signs exerts any influence. The section in this book entitled 'Who am I?' (p. 12ff) is therefore subdivided into three decades, so that according to your birth date, you can easily find the information which is relevant to you.

There is also a second important cosmic defining feature, namely your ascendant. This is the sign of the zodiac that was to be seen on the eastern horizon at the exact time you were born. The ascendant strengthens, weakens or varies the definition of your sun sign, which is why we go into it in greater detail later in the book (p. 49ff). You can learn how to find out your ascendant on page 82ff.

While the Native American horoscope resembles our Western horoscope in that it is divided into twelve, the Chinese and Celtic horoscopes differ, which is why you will find that the information in these sections is subdivided according to dates of birth.

Publisher and Author

Contents

A depiction of the zodiac on a Persian
bowl dating from around 1563.

Messahalah, the astronomer, 1504.

I.
How I am Influenced by Cosmic Affairs

My Sign of the Zodiac and My Planet

Your sign of the zodiac is Pisces, your planet is Neptune, or traditionally called Jupiter.

Pisces is a changeable water sign with minus-polarity. Changeable are the signs of weak intensity and energy spreading towards width. The sign of Pisces symbolises sensitivity, idealism, adaptability, reserve, imagination, intuition, the ability to sacrifice and renounce, acquiescence, but also extreme passivity and lack of energy resources and persistence. As a sign assigned to the element of water it stands for passive actions (key term 'insight'), strong emotions, sensitivity, striving towards protective seclusion from the outer world. The main characteristics thus defined are caution, reserve, the ability to renounce, but also lability and inner insecurity. The polarity determines the effective direction of a sign. Positive signs work from the inside out, negative signs work from the outside in. Pisces is a sign with minus-polarity, i.e. a 'passive' sign symbolising a waiting disposition towards the environment, taking it in.

The basic astrological qualities of the winter sign Pisces can be summarised under the key term of 'introverted perception of the world'. In detail the sign symbolises reserve, sensitivity, idealism, strong imaginative power and intuition, adaptability and empathy with others, but also a lack of assertion and missing energy resources as well as excessive passivity. If not only the sun, but also the ascendant is positioned in the sign at the moment of birth, this will define the personality particularly strong.

Jupiter – also called Neptune – on a cart, the wheels of which represent the domiciles of Pisces and Sagittarius. Wood-carving by Hans Sebald Beham, 1530/40

The planet whose principle most strongly corresponds to each sign of the zodiac has been assigned to that sign; the respective planet is called 'dominating planet'. The sign of Aquarius is 'dominated' by Neptune, whose energetic principle is the power of imagination. It symbolises emotional sensitivity, impressability, sensibility, altruism, the ability to make sacrifices, inspiration, but also deception and self-deception, illusion and disintegration.

If Neptune appears in your personal horoscope of the sun sign Pisces, it will enhance Neptune-characteristics according to likely determining factors of your sign and therefore essentially determine the 'basic quality' of your sign.

Positive Neptune-qualities are: strong sensitivity, immediate sensual contact with the environment, introspectiveness, the willingness to make sacrifices, subtle tact, empathy, perception of profound connexions, an intuitive perception of subtle undercurrents, imagination and fantasy, deep emotions, an appreciation for arts, altruism, creative inspirations, an interest in higher values and a psychological talent.

Negative characteristics of Neptune are: a strong dependency on influences from the outside, a lack of individual distance, insecurity, indetermination, passivity, surrender to illusions, a tendency towards deception and self-deception, susceptibility to seduction and suggestions, a lack of endurance and assertion, psychic irritability, risk of escaping into a dreamworld and distraction through addictive substances (such as alcohol, nicotine or drugs).

In former times different symbols used to be brought into connexion with each astrological sign and planet, which no longer have much meaning for today's individual astrology. However, many people are still interested in those symbols. The following are the symbols connected with your sign:

Your element is water.
Your colours are blue, white, violet, iridescent colours.
Your temper is melancholic.
Your metals are platinum and pewter.
Your precious stones are chrysolite, saphire, topaz, opal, mother-of-pearl, crystals.
Your day of the week is Thursday.
Your animals are all animals of the water, such as fish, whale, crocodile, jelly-fish, shells, seal, swan, seagull, but also lizard and chameleon.
Your plants are rush, water-lily, weeping willow, mushrooms, poison and narcotic plants (such as nicotine, opium), Christmas rose.
Your number is three.

Who am I?

Fundamental principles can be deducted from the position of the sun on the day of your birth; however, these should take your ascendant (see Page 49 and Part III of this book) into consideration. The prologue on Page 5 informs you about the division of each astrological sign into three decades. Depending on whether you were born during the first, second or third decade, the various 'typical' defining energies affect your sun sign differently.

Astrologer.
Taken from a Book of the Planets, 1596.

1st Decade: from 19 February to 1 March

Your nature:	emotional, introverted, sensitive, reserved, helpful
Your manner:	cautious, distant, friendly, sometimes self-conscious, distrustful, soft
Your wishes:	striving for harmony, willing to adapt, lacking ambition, changing goals, indecisive, influenceable
Your way of thinking:	imaginative, intuitive, often creative, not systematic, sometimes without an opinion, acquiescent, unrealistic
Your actions:	cautious, with a sense of duty, peaceful, caring, little energy and persistence, sometimes evasive and unreliable
Your style of speaking:	reserved, illustrious, emotional, cautious, sometimes vague and inconsistent
Your emotions:	sensitive, romantic, emotional, imaginative, willing to make sacrifices, sometimes moody, sentimental, sensual, passionate

You are usually an introverted, emotional and sensitive individual, i.e. what is called a 'delicately-strung' mind. Since you are mainly focused on your inner world, you do not develop strong activities on the outside, only rarely spontaneously approach your environment and other people and cautiously keep your distance. You do not try to be in the limelight und don't enjoy being the centre of attention. When dealing with others, you are polite and friendly, pleasant, adaptable and helpful, but you often appear insecure, shy and soft-spoken even though you sometimes know how to hide that under a distinctly self-assured appearance and with the help of a natural acting talent. You are not expressly decisive; your energy potential is limited, and therefore you don't assert yourself very well; your willingness to perform and your endurance are also limited. You try to avoid any difficulties and disputes that drain your energy; you usually choose the path of least resistence, not because you are cowardly or lazy, but rather because you are aware of the fact that you don't have hard elbows and would most likely be defeated. However, you tend to underestimate your possibilities, have less confidence in your potential than you really are capable of, and often don't even try to test your chances.

However, if you were born at the very beginning of the first Pisces-decade and are therefore still partly under the influence of the preceding sun sign of Aquarius, you show more self-esteem, ambition and persistence, since that influence has a stabilising effect on you and reduces your overly cautious reserve. It makes you more independent and self-assured, but even then the characteristics typical for Pisces will always dominate.

You do have an alert mind, but your whole being is mainly emotional. You are very sensitive and have a fine instinct as well as the gift of intuitive perception, which allows you to gain insights and experience a world hidden to the purely mind-oriented person. You perceive subtle undercurrents, can often sense developing tendencies in advance, sense connexions and possibilities. However, you are often unable to gain personal advantage from your talents, since you lack the energy to transfer perceptions into deeds vigorously and thus benefit practically from them. With your thin skin and inner insecurity you often have difficulties to accept the rough reality and to assert yourself in the tough battle of life. Whenever you face resistance and problems, you tend to get discouraged and give up prematurely; the peace-loving individual striving for harmony and balance that you are makes you no fighter. When you feel overly challenged, humiliated or not appreciated, you tend to escape reality, which is made easy by your strong concentration on yourself and your rich imagination: you then create a world of dreams and wishful thinking that is so much more pleasant and comforting than the harsh real world. Often you abuse alcohol or drugs to help you escape reality, which can more or less quickly lead to regular self-destruction. Such evasive behaviour will solve not one single problem. You can only succeed in life if you face it, and when you feel challenged and threatened by reality too much, the support of a more stable, realistic person will be far more helpful than a useless escape which often does nothing but enhance and increase problems.

Though your energy potential is limited, you can achieve a whole lot with the help of your talents and skills when you face tasks that suit you and which you are familiar with. Even though you are not overly ambitious, you do develop a considerable willingness to work if your self-esteem is strengthened by praise and recognition. Often, however, you contribute to the fact that acknowledgement remains absent, since you like to stay in the back, are overly modest, avoid any tough competition, so that your achievements are either overlooked or undervalued. You react very nervous to any kind of coercion; you usually don't even try to fight it and take the initiative to change the given situation or at least make the best out of it. However, if you accept everything passively, approach circumstances with apathy and let others push you into the background, you will never be able to show what you really are made of. Particularly if you were born at the very beginning of the first Pisces-decade and are therefore still under the influence of Aquarius, you are most definitely capable of showing resolution instead of just being pushed around. Do it and you will see that the success you achieve with that new attitude will make you more self-assured and will increase your self-esteem!

For short periods of time you are definitely able to mobilise a strong willpower and considerable energy, but you usually cannot keep it up for long, specially if you run into obstacles and problems. You don't finish everything that looked promising when you started it, because you lack tough persistence and ambition. You often don't set your goals very high, since you have too little confidence in yourself, or you split your interests and energy, have several projects running at the same time and thus lose control due to lack of concentration. Your material benefits rarely form the centre of your interests, but your need for security can cause you to make quite an effort to earn money. The stability of your financial basis, however, is endangered by the fact that you are not always good with money and often are too generous to yourself and others. It would probably be to your advantage if your partner or spouse could calculate more soberly than youself, so that money and property can be kept together and grow. Doubtlessly a fat bank account that makes you forget money worries can soothen you tender nerves and contribute to your self-confidence.

You are an emotional being who mainly perceives the world through feelings and senses delicate nuances hidden to the average person. Your sensibility usually makes you appreciative of arts: you love music, fine arts and poetry and can be strongly impressed. You are unable to grow a thick skin around your psyche. You get hurt easily and feel sorrow and pain more intensely than others. You therefore frequently have a profound fear of physical and mental pain and sometimes even develop exaggerated anxiety complexes. On the other hand you are literally able to feel with others and can suffer the pain of others as intensely as your own. That makes you sensitive and helpful, but even though you can comfort others and make sacrifices, you rarely are a strong and reliable support due to your inner insecurity and lability, and in the end your giving nature is not completely selfless, since you secretly expect gratitude and recognition to enhance your self-esteem.

Your emotionality makes you susceptible to mood changes manifesting themselves as moodiness. With that you don't only get on some people's nerves, but you also restrict yourself in your actions, upset yourself emotionally and have difficulties to keep yourself under control. Failures lead to disappointments, and if you subsequently give up and escape into your dreamworld, your situation becomes more and more tricky. Make an effort to control yourself as much as possible; here a stabilising partner can be of great help. However, you must be ready to open up to him/her without any restraints, and that is hard for you, since you are very apt in covering up negative situations with the acting talent you most likely have. Even if you don't take the profession of acting, you do like to play roles you chose yourself, in which you pretend quite a lot to others as well as to yourself, so that sometimes you are no longer able to keep make-believe and reality apart.

Though you are no bundle of excessive energy and constancy, no fighter, you can still achieve more than you usually believe yourself. Fight your anxiety and insecurity, divide your goals into controllable and realistic steps, the reaching of which will enhance your self-esteem and give you mental motivation. That way you will gain the security step by step that enables you to face reality and do justice to the challenges of life.

2nd Decade: from 2 March to 10 March

Your nature:	introverted, emotional, sensitive, idealistic, reserved
Your manner:	friendly, good-natured, distant, inconspicuous, sometimes insecure and self-conscious
Your wishes:	helpful, adaptable, peaceful, often lacking ambition, sometimes inconsistent
Your way of thinking:	imaginative, intuitive, not very methodical, even unconcentrated, unrealistic, unclear
Your actions:	cautious, selfless, conscientious, often indecisive, lacking endurance, evasive, unsystematic, unreliable
Your style of speaking:	emotional, reserved, illustrious, considerate, sometimes vague and unclear
Your emotions:	profoundly emotional, warm-hearted, sensitive, imaginative, romantic, sometimes effusive, sentimental, melancholic, moody

Being a Pisces, you are mainly an emotional individual in tune with your inside. You do have an alert intellect, but basically perceive the world with the help of your feelings and intuition, and that perception and experience enable you to sense depths and nuances hidden to the average person around you. You are extremely sensitive and with your fine instinct can perceive subtle undercurrents, notice connexions and often sense tendencies a mainly mind-oriented person has no antenna for. However, you often are unable or unwilling to personally gain from that ability, since you lack the energy to act on your perception. You benefit from your sensibility in human relationships, because it enables you to feel for and understand others. You also owe your appreciation of arts, music and poetry to your sensitivity, which often drives you to creativity.

That can lead to disappointments which can turn your natural reserve into distrustful distance, so that you may approach even those who mean well with suspicion. You are not able to grow a thick skin that would protect your psyche and make you less vulnerable. You are and always will be relatively sensitive and suffer disappointments, sorrow and pain less well than other people. For that reason you often have a deep fear of physical or mental pain and sometimes you even drive yourself to anxiety complexes. That sensitivity, however, also enables you feel true empathy with others: you experience the sorrow of others as intensely as it it was your own. You can feel profound compassion for others and are thus able to comfort and support them when they suffer. Your helpfulness is less efficient in regards to practical problems, though, since you more often than not helplessly face those in your own life.

Since you are mainly emotional, you are susceptible to mood changes you can control only with difficulty; therefore you often appear moody and hardly calculable. This instability burdens not only your relationships with others, but also yourself, since your mood changes between exaggerated euphoria and depressed pessimism is very strenuous for your nerves.

Being a Pisces, you usually only have a limited energy potential. That is why you use your energy frugally, don't set your goals too high or push into the limelight and are not particularly persistent. You often don't only lack the will to assert yourself, but also determination, willingness to perform and tough perseverance. You avoid difficulties and stressful disputes wherever possible; if you can, you will avoid obstacles since you know that you often lose a tough battle. You are no natural fighter; you are peaceful and strive for harmony and balance. Resistance and obstacles discourage you and make you give up prematurely. Since you are a particularly sensitive individual, you often find it hard to stand up to the demands of harsh reality and face the hard competition in our competitive society. If you feel too coerced, over-exerted, treated unfairly or misunderstood, you tend to escape into your own world, which is far more pleasant and comfortable than harsh reality. Numerous Pisceans also abuse alcohol or drugs as 'helpers' to escape – and that is very hazardous, since it can lead to self-destruction. Should you run that risk you definitely need to self-reflect and turn around with determination. If you are unable to face the tough realities of life by yourself, you should seek the assistance of an understanding, stable and realistic individual or a group of peers, instead of suffering alone out of false pride and perhaps even ruin your life.

Your idealism has two sides as well. You can get enthusiastic about ideals and actively commit yourself as long as you see a realistic chance to realise them; you don't care for vague Utopian ideas. But in your impulsiveness, which often is ill-considered, you risk turning into an ideological activist who gets on the wrong track and aims way too far.

You have no reason for resignation, because in spite of your limited energy potential you definitely are capable of considerable achievements, particularly if you take on tasks that suit you and your talents. Recognition and praise serve as important motivation for your willingness to perform. The fact that you don't always get what is due to you is, at least partly, your own fault: you stay in the shadows too often and greatly underestimate your own abilities. When things don't develop as planned, you rarely become active to effect a change. As long as you remain so passive, you can never show what you are really made of. Stand up, accept challenges and, most important: have more confidence in yourself! Only if you take on that attitude can you experience success that will stabilise your self-esteem. You are capable of doing that, since you can very well mobilise strong willpower and considerable amounts of energy while concentrating on a certain task. It can be of great help if you have the support of a more ambitious partner; such support will often also stabilise your material basis, something you pay too little attention to. You are not very good with money; on one hand making money is rarely the focal point of your interests, and on the other hand you find it hard to keep your earnings together, because you are too generous to yourself and others.

However, you don't make it easy for people who mean well to help you. When you have problems, you often retreat into your world of dreams and at the same time use your natural acting talent, pretend to others (and often even to yourself) that things are different and hide your true situation, so that your needs are covered up. From most people around you you cannot expect the fine sense for the needs of others that is given to you. More openness towards your environment in these situations is therefore advisable.

You place great value on a harmonious atmosphere in your private as well as in your professional life. For that reason you try not to let any tensions arise or remove them as quickly as possible and make compromises, make cuts or, if necessary, waive your claims. However, don't be too acquiescent, because otherwise you run the risk that others confuse your reserve with cowardly weakness and try to take advantage of you and abuse you more or less shamelessly. Don't be too moderate in the initial setting of your goals; if you divide your goals into controllable steps that are adapted to your means, you will achieve a series of successful experiences that motivate your ambition and enable you to realise higher and higher goals in due time. Have courage and confidence in yourself! Your cosmic definition has equipped you with a lot of positive talents and abilities: prove to yourself and to those around you what you are made of and what you are able to achieve. It just might surprise you to learn how much that is.

3rd Decade: from 11 March to 20 March

Your nature:	emotional, introverted, reserved, sensitive, imaginative
Your manner:	distant, good-natured, cautious, sometimes evasive and vague
Your wishes:	sincere, willing to adapt, peaceful, often lacking ambition and goal-orientation, sometimes overly worried and inconsistent
Your way of thinking:	creative, imaginative, sensible, directed by emotions, influenceable, sometimes illogical, unrealistic, not concentrated
Your actions:	careful, conscientious, helpful, generous, not very decisive, sometimes lacking persistence, not methodical, easy-going, not very thorough
Your style of speaking:	emotional, imaginative, reserved, inspired, sometimes eloquent and vague
Your emotions:	profound, deep, warm-hearted, sensitive, romantic, sometimes moody, inconsistent, sentimental, melancholic

The astrological sign of Pisces symbolises cautious reserve, acquiescence, sensitivity, imagination, sympathy, idealism, helpfulness, intuition and emotional dependence, but also a lack of energy and endurance, passivity and insecurity. Being a Pisces, you are introverted, i.e. mainly focused on your inner world, rarely spontaneously approach your environment and those around you, but rather wait passively in order to adjust to the given situation with an alert intellect and intuition. You don't push to the front, do not want to be the centre of attention, but you do desire acknowledgement and recognition. The fact that you don't always receive the honours you deserve is to a great part your own fault: your modest distance tends to let you stay in the shadow of life, be pushed into the back so much that your achievements are overlooked or that others might even get the praise you deserve. You only show more self-esteem and assertion if you were born at the very end of the third Pisces-decade and are therefore partially under the influence of your neighbour sign of Aries, which endows you with greater power and energy.

You are extremely sensitive, are able to recognise depths and shades of life that remain hidden to the pure mind-oriented person, can perceive subtle undercurrents, see hidden connexions and sense future developments in advance. You mainly perceive the world through your emotions and are strongly dependent on your emotions in all aspects of life. That, however, also effects a susceptibility for emotional mood changes that you have difficulties to control or soften, so that rather abrupt changes between exaggerated euphoria and depressed pessimism are not the exception for you. You don't only unnerve others with your moodiness, but it also burdens you yourself, because it can put a serious strain on your human relationships and greatly impair your activities in the outer world.

Your dependence on your emotions makes you impressable but also easily influenceable. You usually appreciate music, arts and literature, are often endowed with a talent for arts or acting and use your talent either professionally or as recreation. You are also open to the beauty and secrets of nature, plants, animals and landscapes. You may very well enthusiastically enjoy gardening in your spare time or even make it your profession. Your susceptibility to being influenced, coupled with your acquiescence based on your peace-loving nature, can be to your disadvantage, if others abuse those qualities and try to cheat you or take advantage of you. Often you are too trusting and not critical towards those around you, particularly if these are more or less close friends. For that reason you will again and again encounter a more or less shameless abuse of your trust. In the long run that can make you become distrustful and not open towards others, so that you will finally approach even those who mean well with suspicion. You can avoid quite a few disappointments if you are more critical from the start.

Your sensitivity endows you with great empathy, an ability which serves you well when dealing with others. You literally feel with others, since you feel someone else's sorrow as deeply as if it was your own. The problems of others can become a burden to you, but you are unable to grow a 'thick skin'. Because of your sensitivity you suffer disappointments and sorrow more profoundly, feel pain more deeply than others. Sometimes you develop regular anxiety complexes in anticipation of physical or psychological suffering. You should most definitely attempt to stop such a development early on; here the support from sympathetic persons can be very valuable.

The energy potential available to you is limited. Since you sense that or have learned that fact early on, you usually use your energy sparingly. You do not set your goals very high and choose the path of least resistance wherever possible, avoid obstacles and stressful disputes. You don't have particularly strong elbows, are no natural fighter. You mainly show patience and persistence while waiting for a promising opportunity, but apart from that you usually gather little toughness and tenacity. Your caution hinders you from making quick decisions. You are easily discouraged by difficulties and obstacles and then give up prematurely. Tough competition does not suit you at all; you prefer communication to arguments and strive for harmony and consonance. However, if you were born at the end of the third Pisces-decade and therefore are already under the influence of Aries, that will make you less ready to compromise and more self-assured and assertive.

But even then you will often show a tendency characteristic for Pisceans: the tendency to withdraw from the harsh real world after failure or disappointments and escape into a world of wishes and dreams. Your rich imagination supplies you with that comforting realm, but your escape from reality is often enhanced by alcohol or drugs that enable you to 'switch off' the unpleasant outer world even more effectively. That tendency is obviously not restricted to Pisceans, but they are particularly at risk due to their lability and mental sensitivity. You should therefore be careful and consider that you diminish your health with such toxic substances that will destroy you in the end. The escape from reality solves none of your problem, but only grants a highly illusive postponement and usually increases problems. Muster the courage to face the facts and to work with them, even if you find that hard to do. A better help than addictive substances are understanding, stable individuals who encourage and support you. However, you must give them the opportunity to help you; you must not attempt to cover up your situation with the aid of your natural acting talent, you must not delude them and yourself, but you must admit honestly and without any false pride that you need their help. You yourself don't hesitate to support others in need – so look for a strong shoulder to lean on when you need support yourself!

The fact that you keep getting into those situations is also your own fault, however, since you often are too fearful, give up too quickly and give yourself less credit than you should. Even though your energy potential is limited, you can achieve considerably more than you think and are able to mobilise astonishing amounts of energy and surprisingly strong willpower, at least for shorter periods of time. If you relax and dare to make full use of your abilities and opportunities, you can definitely apply your power to achieve the success that will motivate you further and nourish your self-esteem. So don't be too modest, don't 'sell' yourself under value, show yourself and others what you really are capable of! Once you have overcome your insecurity and discarded your excessive passivity, you can achieve things that will surprise others. Stand on your feet and show more confidence in what you can do! This will be easier for you if someone who means well, perhaps a family member or your partner, gives you sensitive support without pushing and coercing you and thus helps you gain more self-assurance.

So you have no reason at all to feel or act like a wallflower; you don't need to let others push you into the back, you should not let your doubts and exaggerated fears put obstacles between yourself and your possibilities. Set yourself realistic goals and divide the road leading there into controllable sections, so that you repeatedly experience partial successes that will motivate you over and over again. You will see that you can realise even high-flying plans that way. Do not evade reality even if it is everything but pleasant at times. You cannot solve problems if you run from them, but only if you face them head on.

My Predisposition

You are an introverted human being mainly focused on your inside; you are endowed with an alert mind but basically emotion-oriented. You approach your environment and other people with cautious reserve that often lets you appear shy and self-conscious. You are not very self-assured by nature and therefore need successful experiences that bring you attention and recognition and stabilise your self-esteem. However, you sometimes make it difficult for yourself to get that motivation, since you do not have much confidence in yourself and try to stay in the back, if possible; you don't feel comfortable being the centre of attention. Because of your limited energy potential your persistence is not very high and you give up prematurely when encountering difficulties and obstacles. You are easily hurt emotionally and lack self-assertion. Disappointments and failures drive you into a world of dreams and wishful thinking that you created with your rich imagination to escape harsh reality.

You are endowed with intuition that lets you perceive nuances hidden to the purely mind-oriented person. Because of your sensitivity you can feel real empathy for others and are able to support them in their emotional pain, but you face practical problems rather helplessly. Your sensitivity lets you appreciate music, arts and poetry; you often have an artistic or acting talent. You even enjoy playing roles in everyday life and like to pretend to others and yourself; that way you cover up and postpone the problems you have without solving them. You find it difficult to face the harsh reality of life; self-doubts often hinder you from realising the whole range of your positive gifts and talents.

That basic disposition determined by the sun sign already shows in young Pisceans. They are very emotional and sensitive, but usually lack inner stability so that their fluctuation of emotions shows as moodiness. They are expressly thin-skinned; when encountering any problems, they tend to escape into a fantasy world where they seek comfort. Since the child's problems are not solved or disappointments processed that way, the parents should try to help their child as early as possible to face reality and cope with unpleasant situations. It is important to strengthen the child's self-esteem, which can be enhanced by experiences of success in areas the child has a particular talent in (singing, music, painting, crafts etc.). It is necessary to motivate young Pisceans to get involved in goal-oriented activities, since they often are rather passive and lethargic and rarely take the initiative.

Careful encouragement presupposes close contact, so that the child opens up trustingly, because it is by nature rather reserved and shies away from disclosing its needs or problems. In addition a young Pisces may also have a natural gift for acting and is able to cover up problems and delude its environment about its true mental condition. Well-directed encouragement therefore requires a lot of intuition. Any extreme shyness should also be reduced in order to make it easier for the child to socialize and become part of a community. Most useful and particularly important for single children is meeting peers at an early age, so that the child will overcome its shyness and self-doubts and gain self-esteem and openness by being with others in a relaxed environment.

If that works, then young Pisceans will have less problems at school. However, the parents will often not be very happy with their child's grades. The child is intelligent, but not very ambitious and not very performance-oriented. Usually the problem is not the inability to learn, but the lack of willingness to study: the child is mainly interested in subjects that stimulate imagination and feelings, but it finds it hard to think abstractly and logically-systematically. A good relation to the teachers can enhance the child's willingness to learn; a frequent change of teachers or schools will reduce the child's performance. Reproach or even penalties will not result in better grades; encouragement and instructions for goal-oriented studying are much more efficient.

In former times it was common in astrological literature to assign certain professions to each astrological sign, supported by ancient symbolic relations. Today's professional life no longer allows for such a generalisation, because in the last decades the working life has changed a lot and numerous professions have undergone strong changes. By taking these facts into consideration, an astrological career counseling must therefore be adapted to the individual case based on an individual horoscope precisely calculated and analysed. In this chapter we only consider the determination by the sun sign, and for that reason we have to contend ourselves with general indications.

The sensitivity and helpfulness typical of Pisceans lets many of them tend towards medical and nursing professions, as well as social work, psychology and psychiatry. If they take up those professions, they are willing to subject themselves to a discipline and control they can hardly endure in any other situation. Other services of a social nature are also popular among Pisceans. An artistic talent can lead to music, poetry, painting or acting, which does not have to be realised professionally, but can also be taken up as a recreational activity. The love for nature can also express itself as a hobby (gardening etc.) or in the choice of profession (florist, animal caretaker etc.). Traditionally all professions are assigned to the sign of Pisces which have to do with bodies of water or liquids, from navigation to fishing and from the industry processing beverages to gastronomy.

Pisces are usually not overly ambitious, but they do strive for attention and recognition. They do not push into the limelight and dislike being the centre of attention; due to that reserve their achievements are not always honoured as deserved. Tough competition does not suit them; in order to avoid tensions and arguments they prefer to cut back on their claims. Their plans and activities are not always realistic, since wishful thinking can play a considerable role in their lives. They are troubled by mood changes that they often can hardly control or soften. Their personal and professional relationships also strongly depend on their emotions; sympathy and a harmonious work climate have an effect on Pisceans that increases their performance. They sometimes lack ambition and persistence, and their hesitating indetermination can also hinder them. Their intuition, however, often proves very valuable by offering them profound insights and surprising solutions. Since Pisceans can be strongly influenced positively as well as negatively, it definitely is possible to motivate them in their careers by encouraging them to stabilise their self-esteem and by keeping them from giving up prematurely when they encounter difficulties. Once they have gained self-confidence and have had successful experiences, because they have dared something, have shown confidence in themselves, they can get very far on their own, because their new-found self-confidence starts a 'chain reaction' that wakens their ambition and enhances their ability to perform, and each new success contributes to the stabilisation of their climb on the professional and social ladder.

My Health

When, in former centuries, a famous, high-ranking personality fell ill, not the physican but the astrologer was called in first; he had to give important advice to the doctor for his diagnosis and treatment. A lot of physicians, however, were astrologers themselves, such as Paracelsus, the most eminent physician at the turn of the middle ages to modern times, who held the opinion that the observation of the celestial constellations was an important prerequisite for any successful treatment. At the time that had been common practise for milleniums, as evidence from Greek and Roman antiquity shows.

The assignment of certain body parts, organs and illnesses to astrological signs and stellar constellations is ancient as well All it means is that according to the constellations of the horoscope certain weaknesses and dangers are given. However, it does not mean that such illnesses and injuries have to occur: a disposition towards certain illnesses and injuries evidenced in the birth horoscope only then becomes dangerous if during the course of life certain stellar constellations activate dormating dispositions. It should not be concluded from that fact that 'the stars make you ill'; they don't produce diseases, just as a clock does not 'make' time. Clocks indicate the time and star constellations show threatening dangers. So if I heed those warnings in time, am familiar with my weak points and know the dangers, I can take counter-measures to avoid them. I can then change my lifestyle and nutrition, stay away from unhealthy stimulants, strengthen my organism through exercise, gymnastics, water therapy according to Kneipp, etc. and thus ensure that my disposition towards certain diseases does not turn into actual illnesses.

Assigned to the sign of Pisces are the feet as well as the breathing and digestive organs, the lymph system and nerves, which indicates not only a susceptibility of the feet, but also a whole range of slow and chronic illnesses; at an older age circulation problems and a weak heart are also possible. The 'dominating planet' in the sign of Pisces is Neptune, to which the sun system and the pineal gland are assigned. There is a general risk of psychosomatic illnesses, i.e. illnesses caused by psychological problems, some of which are difficult to diagnose. Based on the personality structure a greater health risk through alcohol or drugs is also possible.

The traditional medical assignments of astrology are not made accidentally or exclusively based on symbols at all, even though symbolic thinking certainly played an important role in former times; they are the result of milleniums of careful observation and connexions between terrestrial and cosmic events.

Proclivities and Prevention

The indicated dangers you are prone to do not signify at all that it is your inevitable fate to suffer such illnesses; they rather mean that you should be particularly careful in those areas of health, so that your disposition does not turn into injurious reality.

Basically that has little to do with astrology, but simply is a law of common sense. For instance, if you know you have a weak stomach, you will automatically make sure you don't overload it or eat food that is hard to digest, since you know the result from painful experience. You may not be as clearly aware of the dangers indicated in your horoscope, but they must be taken just as seriously. The value of your horoscope is that it offers information about your physical and mental characteristics and dispositions, therefore also about your physical and mental health and any possible impairments. If you know your weak points, you can battle them successfully and take preventive measures that ensure that these dispositions won't lead to actual illnesses and injuries. We have to limit ourselves to general indications, however, since astrological medicine or medical astrology is an extremely complicated empirical science whose methods of diagnosis and therapy cannot be depicted on a few pages.

The Signs of the Zodiac and Their Corresponding Parts of the Body

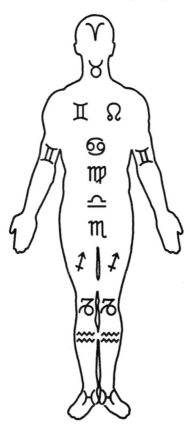

♈ Aries: Head
♉ Taurus: Throat and Neck
♊ Gemini: Lungs and Arms
♋ Cancer: Chest and Stomach
♌ Leo: Heart
♍ Virgo: Intestines

♎ Libra: Kidneys and Urethra
♏ Scorpio: Sexual organs
♐ Sagittarius: Thighs
♑ Capricorn: Knees
♒ Aquarius: Calves
♓ Pisces: Feet

According to traditional astrology you run a greater risk on your feet and through your feet, which means that possible injuries are definitely not restricted to your feet themselves, but also, that your whole organism can be affected by cold or wet feet. Since your breathing organs are also susceptible, they could get infected through colds starting in your feet, but other sensitive body parts can also be affected. Most Pisceans don't have a very sturdy body, and you are therefore susceptible to illnesses caught from your environment.

Mentally you rarely are an example of stability and balance either. You often suffer from inner tensions and conflicts that can express themselves in many physical symptoms; the range of possible psychosomatic illnesses is wide, including even visible organic damages. Such symptoms, however, can also be the result of an escape into illness, which occurs when the feeling of being helplessly subjected to a hostile reality and when the feeling of powerless impotence becomes overwhelming, but relatively often such an escape is used particularly by female Pisceans as a means of blackmail in order to coerce attention or as a punishment for a presumed lack of affection. The motives for such an escape are just as varied as the characteristics of Pisceans are through their cosmic definition.

Besides the escape into illness there also is the escape into a world of dreams and wishful thinking that is cushioned by the rich imagination of Pisceans, so that they believe they can flee from harsh reality. That withdrawal from reality can burden their human relationships, but it can always be overcome as long as the refusal of human contact is not permanent. However, if 'helpers to escape' ranging from alcohol to more or less hard drugs are used, much worse effects must be expected, because this won't only affect a health that is fragile to begin with, but that escape from reality often becomes a habit, too, which is used as a reaction to any stress and demands. If that behaviour has become habitual, the person is no longer able to see that this is no solution but rather a dangerous one-way street that will end in the dissolution of his or her personality structure and often enough in premature death. Frequently a subconscious drive towards self-destruction plays a role in such a development.

Not only in a situation like that, but in general an understanding, sensitive person would be helpful, who can give the Pisces-individual more assurance and steadfastness through his or her own stability and intense attention, so that the Pisces-individual learns to face the facts of life and to cope with their own problems. However, not all representatives of this sun sign depend on such support from others, since the individual characteristics can vary a lot, so that self-assured and independent Pisceans most definitely are no exception to the rule.

My Ideal Partner – Love and Marriage

Some people get along perfectly well from the very start, while others have a difficult time connecting or even tear at each other in open disputes or constantly smouldering conflicts. Similar and contrasting characteristics play a decisive role in human relationships, and since the human personality is to a large part determined by cosmic coining, comparisons between partners on an astrological basis are very popular.

Such concrete comparisons, however, are only then really reliable if based on the precisely prepared and analysed individual horoscopes of both partners. However, the 'tolerance indicator' of two individuals can be deducted from their sun signs, since the sign of the zodiac in which the sun has stood at the time of birth is the most important determining factor of a personal horoscope. Though no exact statements for the individual case can be made from the characteristics derived from the sun sign, such comparisons are still usefull because they can assist in making human relationships more pleasant and less irritating: if you know the strengths and weaknesses of your fellow human beings, you can better adjust to them and avoid quite a few irritations and crises. That obviously goes hand in hand with the fact that you should know as much as possible about yourself, admit to your weaknesses and not succumb to self-delusion. That is why we first comment on your own behaviour in human relationships, before we compare partners according to their sun signs.

Based on the characteristics of the different sun signs a table has been prepared that compares the twelve signs of the zodiac and evaluates the tolerance level in a scoring system of 1 to 6 points. According to said system Pisces are most compatible with Cancer and Scorpio (6 points each), then with Capricorn and Pisces (5 points each) and with Taurus and Sagittarius (4 points each). Connexions with Virgos or Aquarians (3 points each) or with Geminis or Libras (2 points each) are not as compatible, while Aries and Leos only score 1 point and are therefore at the very bottom of the scale of compatibility with Pisceans. That evaluation, however, only applies to fundamental characteristics; in real life Pisceans can get along very well with Aries, but in that connexion both partners will have to work harder than in other combinations to make the relationship harmonious despite serious differences in disposition, while in a relationship with a Cancer most of that harmony is given from the start.

How You Act in a Relationship

Your astrological sign symbolises a variety of characteristics that enhance harmony in human relationships, such as adaptability, empathy, modesty, acquiescence and the willingness to make sacrifices. Your adaptability can go so far that – most Pisceans being natural actors – you play the exact role expected by your environment and partner, as your fine instinct usually tells you. Also on the emotional level you have good prerequisites for a relationship, because you are tender, emotional, imaginative and endowed with a warm sensuality, but once you have found the right partner and put yourself in 'gear', you can forget your self-consciousness and be surprisingly passionate. You adjust to your partner's desires and needs with great sensitivity – an excellent precondition for a harmonious relationship.

You also have a series of characteristics and patterns of behaviour that can burden and disturb a relationship. You basically have a passive nature, let situations and people approach you and rarely take the initiative. The reason for that are your indetermination and insecurity, sometimes also a certain cowardice and laziness. That can cause you to neglect your job, relationship or household, to let yourself drift, to shun stressful duties and responsibilities and, when problems arise, to escape into a world of dreams and wishful thinking that stems from your rich imagination. Your nerves are not particularly strong. Your moods and feelings can fluctuate all the way to uncalculable moodiness. And in addition to that you are extremely possessive due to your strong need for security and therefore very jealous. If you also tend to jam up and be secretive, misunderstandings and tensions can arise that will threaten your relationship. You don't have hard elbows and your perseverance is not too great. In material matters you sometimes are unpractical and disinterested, qualities which do not necessarily serve the financial basis of a relationship well.

When conflicts occur, you are usually quickly prepared to make up, as long as your feelings have not been hurt too much. You suffer when arguments are drawn out; you prefer to make compromises and concessions to end any disputes quickly. Unfortunately that does not always mean that they are really overcome for good, since due to your mood changes conflicts that seem to have been resolved can resurface again and again. Strive for more stability and security, perseverance and constancy. You will succeed if you have the right partner by your side.

Pisces and Aries

The representatives of those two signs completely differ in their attitudes and behaviour. Aries live from the inner towards the outer world, are active, realistic, full of energy, self-assured and optimistic; Pisceans, on the other hand, are turned to the inside, therefore passive, feed on their world of emotions and dreams and often have less self-esteem. At least Pisceans, who are willing to make concessions, are adaptable, and Aries are helpful and understanding. In addition to that their contrasting dispositions can create an immense attraction which often leads to strong erotic ties between Aries' passion and Pisceans' profound emotions. On the practical level a connexion between the two will benefit both as well, since Pisceans get motivation and stability through their self-assured and active partners, while Aries gain more stability and careful consideration. When both partners are able to adjust to each other, they can achieve a happy and durable relationship. The fact that a connexion between them is evaluated rather negatively on the scale of compatibility results from the difficulties that often arise in daily life due to their opposite characters; these difficulties can unnerve both quite seriously and explain why harmonious, longterm Pisces-Aries-connexions are not very frequent.

Pisces and Taurus

Emotional Pisces and warmhearted Taurus get along very well. Both value security as well as the pleasures of life. They usually live together without many problems, since more passive, adaptable Pisceans like to let their Taurus-partner, who is more dominant, take the lead. However, if their partner is too inconsistent, aimless and moody, that can unnerve Taureans, who are more realistic and practically inclined, even though they greatly profit from their partner's intuitive sensitivity. In a relationship it is up to Taurus to make decisions and care for the realisation of material interests. In that aspect the tendency to enjoy life that both have and which can also include a weakness for addictive substances (such as alcohol) Pisceans may have can be dangerous; Taureans should pay attention that that tendency remains within limits that are reasonable and safe for the household budget. In several aspects there are strong contrasts in character, but since most of them complement each other rather well, serious conflicts that endanger the connexion are relatively seldom. When tensions do occur, particularly Pisceans will find it hard to openly discuss them, but both are loyal and understanding, and Pisceans' strong willingness to make compromises makes a reconciliation easier. Often their relationship is stabilised by an erotic connexion that is rarely very passionate, but very loving, so it can bridge quite a few problems.

Pisces and Gemini

Pisces' profound emotional world exerts a strong fascination on extroverted and sociable Gemini, while on the other hand Gemini's interesting wealth of ideas stimulates Pisces' absorbable imagination. Therefore they are usually attracted to each other when they first meet, and as long as their connexion remains non-committed, that attraction will remain. In a close relationship, however, numerous contrasting characteristics will soon show that can be reconciled only with difficulty. Pisceans require security and safety, peace, harmony and reliability, affection and mental 'demonstrations of endearment'. Geminis are completey different: they love risk, the variety of contacts with the outer world, entertainment and specially their personal freedom. The hesitant insecurity and mood changes Pisceans show unnerve them as much as their own restlessness, lack of constancy, repeated unreliability and seemingly shallow sociability bother their Pisces-partner. Therefore any harmonious longterm relationships are relatively rare. However, a strong erotic connexion is possible if Pisceans let go of their insecurity and let their passion flare up. Common projects and goals, where opposite dispositions complement each other well, will strengthen their relationship.

41

Pisces and Cancer

Cancer can be found at the very top of the compatibility scale for Pisces because both have a lot in common. Both care more about comfortable security and stable domesticity than material gain and fame. They are emotionally oriented, softhearted and sympathetic, have a rich imagination but usually little assertion and willpower. In addition to their being soulmates there usually is a strong erotic attraction between the two. All those are good preconditions for a durable connexion, but a close relationship can be endangered by parallel tendencies, such as the tendency of both to escape into a world of dreams and wishful thinking when times are difficult, or their inability to ensure a stable material foundation of their relationship: a constantly low budget can mean a serious burden that could fortify even small disputes. In day-to-day life the more realistic Cancer-partner should take the lead, manage the household budget and pay attention that his or her less stable partner does not take to the bottle when problems occur. Since both tend towards moodiness, it is important to ensure that the life rhythm of both is as harmonious as possible. However, both have empathy and consideration, so that usually any serious tensions can be avoided and conflicts can be removed quickly.

Pisces and Leo

Durable and happy Pisces-Leo-relationships are not as rare as one may assume based on the unfavourable rating on the scale of compatibility. Emotionally profound Pisceans feel drawn to warmhearted, generous, self-assured Leos, not only on the level of feelings but also because they hope to find stabilising support; Leos, on the other hand, are strongly attracted to Pisceans' depth of emotions and tenderness. That explains why, to the astonishment of their environment, many connexions between two partners who are so different in disposition can be unusually harmonious and durable. Precondition, however, is a lot of mutual consideration, something that does not come easy for extroverted and strongly self-focused Leos, which justifies the low scoring on the compatibility scale in the end. In daily life their contrasts can collide strongly, and if Pisceans feel too neglected due to their partner's various outside interests, it is possible that they may swim away quietly and without complaints or warning. Leos, on the other hand, tend to break off the relationship if they miss enough admiration or being the centre of attention, or if their possessive partner's jealousy unnerves them too much.

🐟 *Pisces and Virgo* 🐐

In many aspects the representatives of those two signs (which directly face each other in the circle of the zodiac) are opposite: Virgos are neat and can at times be excessively pedantic, critical, methodical, realistic and objective, Pisceans are rather vague, insecure, aimless, controlled by their emotions and imagination and dreams. Since opposites do attract, however, happy and durable relationships beween Pisces and Virgo are not as rare as could be supposed based on their contrasting dispositions. Pisces' profound emotional world holds a strong fascination for Virgo, and vice versa a less stable Pisces feels safe with a self-assured, sober Virgo. Therefore a first meeting can rather quickly lead to a relationship, but both will probably have rather serious initial difficulties in the daily life of their close relationship, until both have adjusted to one another. Pisces-partners must teach themselves (or be taught) to show more neatness, punctuality and reliability, and Virgo-partners must learn more empathy, compassion and consideration and give their partner the mental 'demonstrations of endearment' that are essential for him or her. Their fairness, helpfulness and loyalty makes it easier for them to adjust and adapt to each other.

🐟 *Pisces and Libra* ♎

The representatives of those two signs are rather different in their behaviour and temper, but they mainly harmonise in their feelings and last not least in the way they experience sexuality. Therefore they can connect rather easily, but a durable relationship that stands the test of everyday life is relatively rare. Extroverted Libra, who depends on a variety of impulses from the outer world, is not the 'homebody' the Pisces-partner, who strives for security, has dreamed of, and will not show give him or her the desired exclusive attention. Even though Libras are willing to make compromises, that helps them little if their overly sensitive partner closes up due to real or supposed neglect and seeks comfort in a world of wishes or dreams. Material problems are not rare in such a relationship, since both partners pay too little attention to a stable financial basis and lack assertiveness, goal-oriented diligence and persistence. However, both are principally prepared to make concessions; serious disputes threatening their connexion are rare, and the frequent strong erotic attraction offsets quite a few opposites, even though it cannot secure the harmony and stability of the relationship.

🐟 *Pisces and Scorpio* ♏

The high rating of that connexion on the scale of compatibility shows that representatives of those two signs have a lot in common. Both are mainly emotionally oriented, are directed towards their inner world and strive for a close connexion. Opposites can complement each other happily: goal-oriented, diligent Scorpio offers security and stability to his or her partner and receives emotional relaxation due to Pisces' tenderness and warmth. Both feel like soulmates and therefore often connect spontaneously in spite of their strong reserve. Most Pisces-Scorpio-relationships are rather durable, even though definitely not completely free of conflicts since their attitudes and behaviour differ in many ways. Active, realistic Scorpios can be bothered by the passive dreaminess of their Pisces-partner, who on the other hand may be overly challenged by Scorpio's intense sensuality. Both have mood changes, and if their life rhythms differ too much, irritations are unavoidable. Scorpios must be careful not to control and 'organise' their partner; Pisceans must strive for a greater sense of reality and determination. However, profound differences are relatively rare due to many likenesses and corresponding attitudes on fundamental issues, so that those connexions are among the most durable of all relationships.

Pisces and Sagittarius

Despite numerous contrasting characteristics happy and durable Pisces-Sagittarius-connexions are not rare. Often it is extroverted Sagittarius, attracted by the profound soul-life of reserved Pisces, who will take the initial step, but Pisceans like to be swept away by Sagittarians' dynamic optimism as well; Sagittarians' feelings can, once they thaw out, ignite into a surprising passion. A deep erotic connexion between representatives of both signs stabilises their relationship, and in practical daily life quite a few of their contrasts complement each other positively. Pisceans' perception is expanded by the worldliness of their partner, their lability is removed by Sagittarians' self-esteem and openness, their passivity reduced by a variety of impulses. Sagittarians, on the other hand, gain greater sensitivity and ability to concentrate. The possessive jealousy of Pisceans can be a problem, just as Sagittarians' great need for social contacts, which can push the relationship into the background, contains risks. Good will and the willingness to understand, however, can bridge all that, and since both partners are basically loyal and ready to make compromises, Pisces-Sagittarius-connexions are markedly stable.

Pisces and Capricorn

Despite essential characteristic differences that connexion is evaluated rather high on the compatibility scale, since there are a lot of similarities on the emotional level. Both are introverted, rather distant and strongly focused on themselves, their feelings are profound and intense. Often Pisceans with their sensitivity make the initial contact, but if a relationship ensues, it is Capricorn who will take the lead. That makes sense in practical matters, since Capricornians are much more goal-oriented and ambitious and therefore able to ensure that the relationship is built on a stable material basis. This way Pisceans receive the desired security and safety and show their gratitude with loyalty and loving care, which again helps Capricornians to open up more and to show their feelings unrestrictedly. Their emotional ties are rarely very passionate, but instead warm and deep, and that explains why two people with such different dispositions can harmonise so well to the surprise of their environment, and why Pisces-Capricorn-connexions, in spite of a considerable conflict potential, are usually longterm. Both partners must expect quite a few irritations and difficulties in their daily relationship, but that can be overcome by loving attention.

Pisces and Aquarius

On the level of their ideas and ideals as well as on the emotional level representatives of those two signs of the zodiac often get along excellently. The originality and extensive worldliness of Aquarians and the profound emotional world of Pisceans can effect a strong mutual fascination that lets them connect quickly. A friendship between them usually is happy and rewarding for both. A committed relationship, however, is a different matter, since numerous opposites in character can lead to irritations and conflicts, and in spite of the deep emotional connexion that often evolves they can be overcome only with difficulty in day-to-day living. Aquarians are unnerved by Pisceans' indetermination, moodiness and aimlessness, while Pisceans are shocked by Aquarians' rather unconventional attitudes and demeanour, and they often feel neglected and ignored because of their partner's many exterior interests and activities. An additional burden on the relationship can be the inability of both partners to take care of a solid material basis of their connexion, so that their household budget will permanently be low. At least both show understanding and loyalty for each other in conflict situations, so that many relationships are durable in spite of occasional problems.

🐟 *Pisces and Pisces* 🐟

Both mainly correspond on the mental, emotional and physical level. In a relationship between two Pisceans the heart and the soul dominate. At the beginning of a connexion there rarely is a great sweeping passion; usually it is a harmony of the souls that evokes the feelings. Tender affection and a feeling of belonging intensifies this connexion, and if both finally open up to each other completely, the smouldering glow may very well turn into a blazing fire. It may very well also occur that both understand each other excellently and feel very close to each other, even though erotic tension does not develop at all or disappears soon, since sexuality does not necessarily rank high in a Pisces-Pisces-connexion. It is not beneficial for a relationship if both have a different emotional and life rhythm, since low mood swings that enhance each other mutually are not particularly advantageous to the relationship. When they encounter differences, both tend to close up and avoid each other; they feel abandoned by their partner, and such situations can lead to quite a few misconceptions and mistakes (such as reaching for the bottle) that will cause inner estrangement. Both are vulnerable, and once they have escaped into their world of dreams, they often lack the energy to approach each other anew. Despite these problems most relationships between two Pisceans are longterm.

The Astrologers, 1596

The Influence of My Ascendant

The ascendant, i.e. the sign of the zodiac that stands at the easterly horizon at the moment of birth, is immensely important because of its strong defining power; in combination with the sun sign it offers the most significant statements that can be obtained from a birth horoscope. Any individual analysis can only be incomplete if the ascendant has not been taken into consideration.

In order to determine your personal ascendant you obviously need to know what time you were born, since all twelve signs rise at the easterly horizon in the course of one day. In the Chapter 'How to Work Out Your Ascendant' you may read how you can convert your time of birth into local time. Then all you need to do is find your ascendant in the graph of your personal date of birth under the calculated time.

49

The ascendant is the basis of statements that are more individual than those merely deducted from the location of the sun; this is due to the fact that, while all humans born between the end of February and the end of March share the sun sign of Pisces, the ascendant is determined by the individual time and location of birth. However, it gains its full meaning only by the exact determination of degree as indicator of that system of houses that, in its function as a 'fine grid', offers completely individual analysing possibilities for all celestial constellations of the birth horoscope. But we must leave the calculations necessary for that and the statements that can be deducted from that to the expert astrologists.

The ascendant influences the definition by the sun sign more or less strongly and can enhance or diminish certain tendencies. You will find out in this chapter how that applies to you.

Ascendant Aries

The influence of that ascendant makes you more open towards your environment, endows you with more dynamic energy and self-esteem and reduces your dependence on your emotions. In spite of your cautious reserve caused by your sun sign a stronger, more goal-oriented will makes you more determined and direct. You have quite a lot of confidence in yourself and rarely let self-doubts make you insecure, and you do not depend too much on recognition from those around you. Failure and disappointments are not easy for you, but you try with great tenacity to overcome them and start anew. Even though you don't have very hard elbows, you definitely do not let others push you aside without resistance, but rather try to maintain your interests and fight unfairness and setbacks. In spite of your limited energy potential you try to carry out any responsibilities you have taken on conscientiously and efficiently. You avoid obstacles and conflicts whenever possible, but if that is impossible, you can gather an astonishing amount of energy. You don't only depend on your alert mind, but also on your sensitive intuition which often gives you valuable assistance when making decisions. You are less often seduced by Utopian wishful thinking than the 'pure' Pisces-type; you usually keep your plans within the limits of your possibilities and that which is practical. Even though too much excitement unnerves you, you don't shy away from social contacts. In your relationship you are sensitive, helpful, very emotional, devoted and considerate and interested in the stability of the connexion.

Ascendant Taurus

You appear calm and reserved, focus strongly on yourself and your immediate environment and rarely push into the limelight. You are pleasant and friendly to others, understanding and helpful, but you open up little, never impose on others and seem to always wish to keep a certain distance. You are more realistic, goal-directed and headstrong than the 'pure' Pisces-type, keep your interests in sight with greater determination and can mobilise a greater energy potential. You show more perseverance and endurance, don't give up prematurely when you encounter difficulties and care not only for the recognition of your achievements but also for an adequate reward, and you pay more attention to the building of a stable material basis of your life. Failure and criticism can temporarily upset your self-esteem, but it is often stable enough to digest such blows. You are principally willing to adjust and rarely insist on your attitudes stubbornly, but your willingness to make concessions is limited, particularly if your own vital interests are at stake. Though you cannot remove your distinct dependence on your emotions completely, you counter-balance that fact with a lot of common sense and it therefore does not have a too great effect, even if your low mood swings repeatedly bother you. In close relationships you show your emotional side; you are very affable and warmhearted, but in your striving for the stability of the connexion also very possessive and often extremely jealous.

Ascendant Gemini

You are distinctly more sociable and communicative than the 'pure' Pisces-type, are more open for impulses from the outside, but also show a greater willingness to approach others. Your flexible and alert intellect reduces your dependence on emotions, but it does not protect you from frequent mood changes that can reduce your activities and burden human relationships. You have neither a large energy potential nor great perseverance at your disposal, so that you sometimes find it difficult to finish your responsibilities properly. Even though you endeavour the attention and recognition of those around you, you do not try to box your way into the centre because you are no natural fighter. You try to avoid obstacles. When you face difficulties and conflicts, you don't oppose them with the full application of your powers, but rather use tactical maneuvres. Then, if you fail, you often give up and try another road. Some of your failures are your own fault, since you overestimate your energy and possibilities and promise more to yourself and others than you actually can achieve. Though you often appear to be optimistically self-confident, you are greatly affected by failures and disappointments and subsequently feel very insecure. That can have an effect on your mood and lead to discontent and moodiness. You are willing to adjust and prepared to make concessions, but you can also be rather thickheaded and tend to be uncalculably inconsistent in your actions and goals.

Ascendant Cancer

You are very introverted, i.e. extremely concentrated on yourself and your immediate environment. Emotions play an important role in your life, influence your mood and therefore your overall behaviour. You react to your environment with cautious reserve, are not very sociable, let situations and people approach you and rarely take the initiative. Your self-esteem is not particularly stable. You have difficulty coping with failures, unfair treatment and disappointments, become insecure and doubt yourself as a result. In such situations you tend to close up and then you sometimes flee from harsh reality and escape into an Utopian world of dreams that dims your perception for that which is realistic and practical. Your willingness to perform strongly depends on the recognition and praise of those around you: if you get neither, there is a danger that you become extremely passive and lose confidence in what you can achieve. You frequently encounter financial problems: the striving for material gain is not on top of your list of priorities; usually you are not very smart in business matters and pay little attention to financial security. You greatly enjoy the beautiful sides of life, where you prefer immaterial pleasures (such as arts, music, etc.) to culinary and sensual pleasures. Your mood shifts can make daily life difficult for you, but it can also put a great strain on your human relationships, where you are a partner with empathy and emotions who needs a lot of affection and understanding but who can also be extremely possessive and jealous at times.

Ascendant Leo

The influence of that ascendant makes you more open to your environment. You are more affable and sociable and appear more determined and self-confident. You insist on keeping your own interests in mind and don't let others push you aside. You strive for the acknowledgement and recognition of those around you and therefore endeavour to get attention, not necessarily through extraordinary achievements, since your energy potential and perseverance are limited. Despite your alert mind you distinctly depend on your emotions and prefer to rely on your intuition rather than on thoughtful analysing. You are not expressly self-critical, which can cause failure through the miscalculation of your powers and possibilities. However, you do not let disappointments discourage you for long, but usually rather start anew after a short break. You have more willpower than the 'pure' Pisces-type, but you show a tendency towards obstinacy and unflexible insistence on your viewpoints. Even though you have a lot of empathy for others, you are not objective at all in your attitudes and judgements due to your strong concentration on yourself. Emotionally you are very vulnerable in spite of the self-confidence you show; unfair treatment and insults hit you hard. You often have difficulties creating a stable material basis for your life, since your own financial benefits are not on top of your list of priorities, and since you are not very business-like and sometimes too generous in money matters. You are a loyal and warmhearted partner who, however, is not always totally reliable.

Ascendant Virgo

You approach your environment with a cautious, critical and almost distrustful reserve, keep a certain distance that lets you assess your situation based on sharp observation before each contact or activity. You do not only rely on your alert mind, but also on your sensitive instinct which enables you to gain intuitive perceptions. You are distinctly more practical than the 'pure' Pisces-type, think and plan more methodically and approach any tasks with systematic consideration. The success you achieve with that technique strengthens your self-esteem which is relatively stable in spite of all restrictions caused by your mood changes. You know rather well what you want and do not make disadvantageous compromises. You balance your limited energy potential with your versatility, flexibility and communication skills. You do not shun responsibilities, but a lack of endurance and goal-orientation as well as obstinacy that is sometimes exaggerated can cause problems for you. Only very seldom do you open up completely; you do not put a great emphasis on close relationships. That coolness which almost comes across as rejection can cost you quite a lot of the sympathy in your profession you have gained from working effectively, but it has an even greater impact on your social life, because it greatly reduces your circle of friends and acquaintances. However, when you are able to really open up to others, your profound and sometimes even passionate emotional world surfaces; then you are a considerate partner who cares for the well-being of both.

Ascendant Libra

You appear reserved, friendly, helpful and considerate, seem obliging and almost softhearted, but you are a sharp, critical observer with a fine sense for subtle and profound things. You give yourself plenty of time for your judgements and reactions, in order to adjust to any given situation. You rarely carry out ill-considered spontaneous actions; you usually act with careful planning to avoid failure and mistakes as much as possible, since you have difficulties coping with failure, which impresses you too much, makes you insecure and doubt yourself. You try to evade obstacles with tactical diplomacy and to defuse conflicts through reasonable compromises. You rarely show hard elbows and determined self-assertion, because your energy potential is limited. To make the most of it you avoid unnecessary 'energy losses' caused by irritation and plan carefully, whereby you are smart enough not to commit yourself too rigidly in order to be able to react flexibly to unforeseen events. You are no thickheaded fanatic who defends his or her point of view under all circumstances. You accept other attitudes and can change your position if the argumentation is well-founded, but you are no opportunist, either. Fairness to yourself and others means a lot to you. You care about harmony and balance, commit yourself to the causes of those who are disadvantaged and reject suppression of any kind. Harmony is also important to you when dealing with others; you endeavour to reduce tensions and an understanding and harmonious interacting with another human being.

Ascendant Scorpio

You are strongly focused on yourself and your immediate surroundings, mainly emotionally oriented and little open towards your environment. Your cautious and sometimes even distrustful reserve creates distance to others, a gap you rarely bridge out of your own initiative. You are not very communicative and carefully protect your emotional world; you only rarely show feelings. In reality, however, you are extremely emotional, but your emotional world troubles you, since you are driven by your desires in many aspects, something which is hard for you to keep under control due to your strongly fluctuating mood. You often concentrate your interests mainly on your professional and social career, whereby you benefit from an energy potential greater than that of the 'pure'

Pisces-type, which endows you with more perseverance and self-assertion. You know how to use your energy efficiently, avoid confrontations and arguments whenever possible, but you can assert yourself and defend your interests rather well in conflict situations. You often appear more self-confident and tougher than you really are, since you have a soft heart and are very vulnerable emotionally and get upset easily. Unfair treatment and intentional grievances hit you hard and can evoke feelings of revenge in you. In a close relationship you are discreet and faithful, helpful and sometimes of passionate emotionality. However, you also are very possessive, restrictive and due to your dependence on emotions often rather trying, moody and not necessarily reliable if under great stress.

Ascendant Sagittarius

The influence of that ascendant relaxes your cautious reserve, makes you more open for impulses and stimulation from your environment and enhances your sociability. It reduces your emotional dependence, but greater inner mobility can also lead to strong moodiness. You are not very stable in your moods nor in your self-esteem, which can be subjected to strong fluctuations according to your momentary emotional condition or as a reaction to the positive or negative response you get from your environment. Accordingly you over and over again tend towards an exaggerated optimistic self-esteem or have much less confidence in your abilities than you should have. Your career goals as well as your private relationships suffer from those mood swings. When you have found inner balance, however, you have a wide range of positive characteristics at your disposal which enable you to act effectively and successfully. You don't only have an alert and receptive intellect, but also a sensitivity that allows you to gain deeper perceptions than a merely analytical mind could gain. You are adaptable and willing to make compromises, show empathy and obliging friendliness towards others and are able to influence them with skillful and tactical eloquence. You can get far without having to use your elbows by applying your personality and methods. Since you care much more about recognition than you do about financial success, you do risk neglecting the creation and safeguarding of a stable material foundation. You would personally and professionally benefit from a partner who is smarter in business matters than you are.

Ascendant Capricorn

You react to others with polite reserve, are less communicative and only rarely express your feelings. Being introverted you direct your interest mainly towards yourself and your immediate environment. You seldom are particularly sociable, even if you greatly value adequate attention from those around you and praise from others extremely motivates your willingness to perform. However, you do not depend on such praise, since you have a greater energy potential, more perseverance and self-assured ambition than the 'pure' Pisces-type. You care a lot about your professional and social career and are willing to work hard and, if necessary, to sacrifice a great part of your social life for that. Your dependence on emotions troubles you, since mood changes have a distinct effect on your actions and plans. Your self-confidence is by far not as stable as you want others to believe; emotionally you are very vulnerable. Setbacks in your activities hit you less hard than unfair treatment, personal injuries and human disappointments. You strive for independence and do not like to accept help, and because of your reserve you usually only have a few close friends you can or want to turn to. You usually achieve a rather stable material basis. You could probably improve your life considerably if you endeavoured to become more relaxed and open to others.

Ascendant Aquarius

Though as an introverted individual you are strongly focused on yourself, your interests definitely are not limited to your immediate personal environment: you actively interact with the community you live in and commit yourself to tasks that the general public benefits from. That enables you more than the 'pure' Pisces-type to have a wide range of social contacts, even though you generally keep a certain distance. You often are an idealist who likes to get enthusiastic about something, but as a practical sense of reality is not one of your strong characteristics, you run a risk of being susceptible to Utopian dreams and ideologies. Even in your personal sphere you tend to escape disappointments and failures through wishful thinking created by your rich imagination. You are not too constant in your goals and let feelings as well as influence from the outside change your direction suddenly and unwisely give up things you already achieved. You show a certain lability in certain aspects: you do not defend your own opinions and viewpoints with determination; not only insight but also external pressure can make you change your position relatively quickly. In practical life that flexibility, however, is often advantageous to you, since you avoid most irritations and conflicts with your ability to adapt and compromise and can thus make the most of your limited energy potential. Sometimes, however, more determination and direction would be good, because if you are too accommodating you provoke others to abuse you or push you aside.

Ascendant Pisces

When the sun and the ascendant meet in the same sign of the zodiac at the time of birth, this will enhance its positive and negative characteristics. You are very introverted, i.e. directed towards yourself and your immediate surroundings. Often you are not only emotionally oriented, but depend on feelings and moods in all aspects of life. You are not very sociable; your demeanour towards your environment is marked by cautious reserve and careful passivity. You let people, matters and events approach you and only rarely take a spontaneous initiative to have an effect on the outer world. You are not very realistic: again and again you are directed by wishful thinking and overestimate your energy and your possibilities. Then, when you experience failure, you tend to escape into the comforting dream world created by your rich imagination. Get out of that vicious cycle by setting yourself realistic goals in manageable, achievable steps which will repeatedly motivate you and allow you successful experiences that affirm your self-esteem. Try to open up more to the world around you, so that people who care about you can recognise your problems and difficulties and can help you. Don't reject such support out of false pride. A partner who keeps your material interests in view more decidedly than you can, who balances your mood swings, stabilises your goals and makes up for your lack of persistence and perseverance would be beneficial to you. And keeping the many positive dispositions you are gifted with in mind, you can most definitely have more confidence in yourself.

II.
How I Link into
the Universe

My Chinese Horoscope

The centuries-old Chinese form of astrology uses a unique system, which makes it impossible to find a one-to-one correlation with our well-known Western astrology. According to the Chinese theory, five factors determine a person's characteristics, abilities and fate: the animal ruling your year of birth, the season, the week, day and hour of your birth. Every year since the sixth century BC has been allocated to one of 12 animal symbols, giving 12 different animal types. A person's character traits and disposition are dependent on the animal ruling the year of their birth. Our Western astrology has no equivalent for the system of seasons, which correlates with the emotions; there are five seasons, each of which is associated with an element. The Chinese system of 24 weeks (each 'week' corresponds to a Western fortnight) influences your behaviour and position in society. Apart from being influenced by the seasons, your emotional make-up is also influenced by the day of your birth. The hour of your birth, which is located at a particular point of time in the daily cycle of the zodiac, determines a person's physical-psychological character traits.

Although the Chinese 'zodiac' is divided into 12, this system is not totally equivalent to the Western astrological system; one can only speak of parallels. You can determine your animal type using the table on the following page and then read about the corresponding characteristics in our summary. Information is also given concerning the cosmic influence which the seasons and the weeks have on your life.

18 Feb. 1912 - 5 Feb. 1913	Rat	
6 Feb. 1913 - 25 Jan. 1914	Ox	
26 Jan. 1914 - 13 Feb. 1915	Tiger	
14 Feb. 1915 - 3 Feb. 1916	Rabbit	
4 Feb. 1916 - 22 Jan. 1917	Dragon	
23 Jan. 1917 - 10 Feb. 1918	Snake	
11 Feb. 1918 - 31 Jan. 1919	Horse	
1 Feb. 1919 - 20 Jan. 1920	Goat	
21 Jan. 1920 - 7 Feb. 1921	Monkey	
8 Feb. 1921 - 6 Jan. 1922	Rooster	
7 Feb. 1922 - 14 Jan. 1923	Dog	
15 Feb. 1923 - 4 Jan. 1924	Pig	
5 Feb. 1924 - 24 Jan. 1925	Rat	
25 Jan. 1925 - 12 Feb. 1926	Ox	
13 Feb. 1926 - 1 Jan. 1927	Tiger	
2 Feb. 1927 - 22 Jan. 1928	Rabbit	
23 Jan. 1928 - 9 Feb. 1929	Dragon	
10 Feb. 1929 - 29 Jan. 1930	Snake	
30 Jan. 1930 - 17 Feb. 1931	Horse	
18 Feb. 1931 - 6 Jan. 1932	Goat	
7 Feb. 1932 - 25 Jan. 1933	Monkey	
26 Jan. 1933 - 13 Feb. 1934	Rooster	
14 Feb. 1934 - 3 Jan. 1935	Dog	
4 Feb. 1935 - 23 Jan. 1936	Pig	
24 Jan. 1936 - 10 Feb. 1937	Rat	
11 Feb. 1937 - 31 Jan. 1938	Ox	
1 Feb. 1938 - 18 Jan. 1939	Tiger	
19 Feb. 1939 - 7 Jan. 1940	Rabbit	
8 Feb. 1940 - 26 Jan. 1941	Dragon	
27 Jan. 1941 - 14 Feb. 1942	Snake	
15 Feb. 1942 - 4 Jan. 1943	Horse	
5 Feb. 1943 - 25 Jan. 1944	Goat	
26 Jan. 1944 - 12 Feb. 1945	Monkey	
13 Feb. 1945 - 1 Jan. 1946	Rooster	
2 Feb. 1946 - 21 Jan. 1947	Dog	
22 Jan. 1947 - 9 Feb. 1948	Pig	
10 Feb. 1948 - 28 Jan. 1949	Rat	
29 Jan. 1949 - 16 Feb. 1950	Ox	
17 Feb. 1950 - 5 Feb. 1951	Tiger	
6 Feb. 1951 - 26 Jan. 1952	Rabbit	
27 Jan. 1952 - 13 Feb. 1953	Dragon	
14 Feb. 1953 - 3 Feb. 1954	Snake	
4 Feb. 1954 - 23 Jan. 1955	Horse	
24 Jan. 1955 - 11 Feb. 1956	Goat	
12 Feb. 1956 - 30 Jan. 1957	Monkey	
31 Jan. 1957 - 18 Feb. 1958	Rooster	
19 Feb. 1958 - 7 Jan. 1959	Dog	
18 Feb. 1959 - 27 Jan. 1960	Pig	
28 Jan. 1960 - 14 Feb. 1961	Rat	
15 Feb. 1961 - 4 Jan. 1962	Ox	
5 Feb. 1962 - 25 Jan. 1963	Tiger
26 Jan. 1963 - 13 Feb. 1964	Rabbit
14 Feb. 1964 - 1 Jan. 1965	Dragon
2 Feb. 1965 - 21 Jan. 1966	Snake
22 Jan. 1966 - 8 Feb. 1967	Horse
9 Feb. 1967 - 29 Jan. 1968	Goat
30 Jan. 1968 - 16 Feb. 1969	Monkey
17 Feb. 1969 - 5 Jan. 1970	Rooster
6 Feb. 1970 - 26 Jan. 1971	Dog
27 Jan. 1971 - 18 Feb. 1972	Pig
19 Feb. 1972 - 2 Jan. 1973	Rat
3 Feb. 1973 - 23 Jan. 1974	Ox
24 Jan. 1974 - 10 Feb. 1975	Tiger
11 Feb. 1975 - 30 Jan. 1976	Rabbit
31 Jan. 1976 - 17 Feb. 1977	Dragon
18 Feb. 1977 - 7 Jan. 1978	Snake
8 Feb. 1978 - 27 Jan. 1979	Horse
28 Jan. 1979 - 15 Feb. 1980	Goat
16 Feb. 1980 - 4 Jan. 1981	Monkey
5 Feb. 1981 - 24 Jan. 1982	Rooster
25 Jan. 1982 - 12 Feb. 1983	Dog
13 Feb. 1983 - 1 Jan. 1984	Pig
2 Feb. 1984 - 19 Jan. 1985	Rat
20 Feb. 1985 - 8 Jan. 1986	Ox
9 Feb. 1986 - 28 Jan. 1987	Tiger
29 Jan. 1987 - 16 Feb. 1988	Rabbit
17 Feb. 1988 - 5 Jan. 1989	Dragon
6 Feb. 1989 - 26 Jan. 1990	Snake
27 Jan. 1990 - 14 Feb. 1991	Horse
15 Feb. 1991 - 3 Jan. 1992	Goat
4 Feb. 1992 - 21 Jan. 1993	Monkey
22 Jan. 1993 - 9 Feb. 1994	Rooster
10 Feb. 1994 - 30 Jan. 1995	Dog
31 Jan. 1995 - 18 Feb. 1996	Pig
19 Feb. 1996 - 6 Jan. 1997	Rat
7 Feb. 1997 - 27 Jan. 1998	Ox
28 Jan. 1998 - 15 Feb. 1999	Tiger
16 Feb. 1999 - 4 Jan. 2000	Rabbit
5 Feb. 2000 - 23 Jan. 2001	Dragon
24 Jan. 2001 - 11 Feb. 2002	Snake
12 Feb 2002 - 31 Jan 2003	Horse
1 Feb 2003 - 21 Jan 2004	Goat
22 Feb 2004 - 8 Feb 2005	Monkey
9 Feb 2005 - 28 Jan 2006	Rooster
29 Jan 2006 - 17 Feb 2007	Dog
18 Feb 2007 - 6 Feb 2008	Pig
7 Feb 2008 - 25 Jan 2009	Rat
26 Jan 2009 - 13 Feb 2010	Ox
14 Feb 2010 - 2 Feb 2011	Tiger
3 Feb 2011 - 22 Jan 2012	Rabbit

Rats

Tempestuous or rash, self-confident or arrogant, like to make a show of themselves, are often good at lots of things and very knowledgeable and like to make others acutely aware of these facts. Find it very difficult to subordinate themselves and often remain caught up in fixed, old ways. Are actually by nature ready to help others, but can only be generous when praise and recognition are certain. Can be quite materially successful.

Oxen

Full of life and drive, determined, often thinking ahead and planning wisely. Set idealistic targets and put a lot of energy into realising them. Tend not to show lots of emotions, although there are many below the surface. On the grounds of their robust, untiring energy, can sometimes be quite exhausting for others.

Tigers

Extremely adventurous, but also with a lot of stamina in getting things done. Exaggerated vehemence can lead to mistakes cropping up. Courage can turn into a dare-devil attitude. Good self-confidence tends to develop into an overestimation of oneself and into egocentricity, which can lead to inconsiderateness. Feelings are usually very strong, but also unstable.

Rabbits

Often of virtually unlimited energy and restless activity. Usually a fan of art and literature. In spite of a somewhat scary dynamism, can be very patient and understanding of others; are actually very unselfish. Can overcome obstacles which would lead to resignation in others.

Dragons

Fearless, avoid neither enemies nor obstacles, as courage, vitality and power are present in abundance. Often put on a gruff and evasive exterior and sometimes have only a few good friends; in their innermost core, however, very sensitive and ready to listen to others' problems and worries. Have to learn to direct their energy and to force themselves to be more self-restrained and measured.

Snakes

Express the large amounts of energy in activities which are usually driven by creative planning. Can come up with many new ideas and bring about new developments using their creative imagination. However, as soon as the activity has become routine and there are no more new ideas about, do not have much staying power required for putting the plans into action. Are capable of deep thoughts and intense emotions.

Horses

A thirst for action which can hardly be contained is expressed in a multitude of activities, which are sometimes begun rashly. When obstacles and difficulties are encountered, interest in the activity quickly subsides and a new one is quickly begun. Violent emotional outbursts are not infrequent, otherwise emotions are more restrained. Others will find such impatience unfair and will be hurt by it.

Goats

Fanatical sense of justice, tend to look for an argument and be vehement. However, only seldomly condone or use violence and try to overcome conflict situations with passive resistance. Stand up for and fight for others and for ideals. Are usually creative and sometimes artistically inclined.

Monkeys

Always full of plans, which are often tackled simultaneously. In many cases an iron will, strong nerves, foresighted planning and a realistic evaluation of the facts lead to success. Should avoid dissipating energy in too many directions at once and concentrating energies into one thing in order not to hurt themselves and others. Usually get out of difficulties without any problems.

Roosters

Exceptionally active and success-orientated, but also very self-focused, tend to be egotistical, talk a lot, moody. Find it very difficult to subordinate themselves. Their directness is good, but can also hurt others. Roosters are well-loved for their eloquence and wit. Often fascinated by all aspects of nature and have a lot of drive. Not always constant in their affections.

Dogs

Full of energy and extremely daring, but not necessarily with any concrete plans or considered. Again and again let themselves be driven to lashing out blindly. Fight for justice and other ideals; like to have a 'mission', which is followed unflinchingly. However, must be careful to plan things better and not to dissipate energies.

Pigs

Full of fighting energy, but with little stamina and assertiveness. Like to stand up for others, but often misjudge situations and tend to draw hasty conclusions and to act rashly. Can have various artistic talents, but usually need the help of others to achieve success and the respect of others.

The Season

Your astrological sign is divided into two Chinese seasons. The season of water runs from December 22nd to March 2nd, while the season of soil starts on March 3rd. You will find a short definition of both seasons.

The element of water is assigned to winter and connected with the north. It is related to rain and the moon, which symbolises tolerance towards others, work, but also fear and anxieties. The favourite colours of water-beings are ultra-marine, silver grey and black, the colours of winter, but also of the depths of the universe; nine is their lucky number.

Light rain refreshens your mind and relaxes your soul; your favourite colours have a calming and regenerating effect on you when you are ill or exhausted; and you will sleep particularly deeply and well if your head faces north.

The season of soil is not assigned to a particular direction and is divided into four phases throughout the year. It contains the weeks of 3-20 March, 4-21 June, 5-22 September and 4-21 December. Soil symbolises centre and balance. Its favourite colour is yellow, its lucky number is five.

Cleansing thunderstorms vitalise you and refreshen your mind; your favourite colour brings you relaxation and revitalisation. You will find your most regenerating sleep in the centre of your bedroom or if your head faces the centre of the room. You consider the human being to be the centre of the universe, which means focusing on yourself, but also self-esteem and self-confidence, a consciousness of your value and power which helps you be help and support to others. If you overcome the risk of egoism, you can have an active and imaginative effect on the outer world and ensure that your environment is in balance for the benefit of all, including yourself.

The 2nd Chinese Week

You were born during the second Chinese week (the Chinese New Year does not coincide with ours), which encompasses the days from 19 February to 5 March. That is the fortnight of rain and rainshower, which determines your dispositions in certain ways.

You are emotional, sensitive and an idealistic optimist, but you often lack energy and endurance. Though you are reliable and conscientious, you sometimes fail in your actions since you do not stand firmly on the ground of given facts, but repeatedly let yourself be diverted by wishful thinking and put greater emphasis on that which you desire than on that which is possible. When you encounter problems, you tend to escape into a dream world where romantic nostalgia can play a great role. Since you often need a strong hand to lead you and show you the way, you are not suited for managerial responsibilities. However, when you take on an obligation or work that interests you, you accept it readily without thinking about your own benefits, and if your idealism is ignited, contrary to your typical disposition you can even commit yourself to a 'good cause' with energy and courage, even become fanatic. That can happen particularly if it concerns the well-being of a community or the interests of others you care about.

Your weaknesses include indetermination, a lack of endurance and little persistence; a certain distance to reality causes problems again and again. Try to fight it, but it probably would be even better for you if you had a person who could give you more self-esteem, a more realistic view free of illusions and more perseverance, and who can furthermore keep your material interests in mind more realistically and energetically than you can.

The 3rd Chinese Week

You were born during the 3rd Chinese week (the Chinese New Year does not coincide with ours), which encompasses the days from 6 to 20 March. That is the fortnight when animals wake from hibernation, which has a certain impact on your characteristics.

You are controlled more by feelings than by your mind, are imaginative and idealistic. Emotionally and mentally you are somewhat unstable; it is hard for you to set firm goals and directly go for them. That is to a great part due to the fact that you can easily be influenced and lack perseverance; you get distracted and when you encounter obstacles, you like to escape into wishful thinking and thus don't progress at all. However, you do have some ambition and learn in time to take the initiative and be more persistent, but the well-being of the community is always more important to you than your own interests; you are not too concerned with personal fame and material success. You are not particularly suitable for managerial positions due to your lack of determination and organisational talent, but you do work well in a team and usually get along excellently with others. Tasks that the public or the environment benefits from suit you best, since your basic idealistic attitude gives you strong impulses when mobilising your energy and skills.

You need personal space in human and professional relationships. You can also find that required feeling of freedom when traveling, something you love doing. You would greatly enjoy a profession connected to a lot of travel. Since you are able to adjust to reality even though you are so introverted, you can assert yourself in life in spite of the weak points mentioned above.

My Native American Horoscope

Even though the Native American astrology is based on an image of the world and the human being that greatly differs from our occidental ideas, it also arrives at insights on humans that are surprisingly similar to the results derived from our own horoscopes. For Native Americans the human being is tied into the universe as well, is part of a tight network of relations and counter-effects that runs through the whole animated as well as the inanimate world.

The most important reference system of our astrology is the circle of the zodiac with its twelve signs that divide the year. According to the Native Americans a person enters a magic circle at birth that contains the whole world. Four sections subdivide the universe, the annual and daily course, and each are symbolised by one animal: east–spring–morning–eagle; south–summer–noon–coyote; west–autumn–evening–grizzly bear; north–winter–night–white buffalo. Our signs of the zodiac correspond to twelve months, to each of which a totem (sign) in the fauna, flora and mineral realm as well as one symbolic colour are assigned.

You Are a Human Puma

You were born under the moon of the Great Winds that basically corresponds to the time frame of our sign of Pisces. Your totem in fauna is the puma, your totem in flora is the plantain, your totem in the mineral realm is turquoise and your symbolic colour is blue-green. You belong to the element clan of frogs whose element is water. Other members of that clan are the woodpeckers

(Cancer) and the snakes (Scorpio). That means that you share many characteristics with those human beings. You were born in winter, the season of *Baboose* (the White Buffalo), guardian of the spirit from the north, who also symbolises the night and the power of renewal and cleansing.

Pumas are mainly controlled by their rich and profound emotional world; they are directed more by their intuition than by their intellect. Their spiritual disposition often goes hand in hand with an artistic talent. They are not particularly realistic; they feel more comfortable within the high and low spheres of their world of emotions and feelings. An inner insecurity and self-doubt cause them to examine any plans and attitudes thoroughly before accepting them; they therefore appear to be indecisive, tentative and lacking activity. Yet they can be very productive once they get going; they are able to be very patient and are conscientious, but they do not have a lot of perseverance and persistence.

Human pumas have to work hard on themselves to gain control of their frequently rather tangled feelings. Therefore they often close up to others, appear friendly and obliging, but remain taciturn and show little emotion. Being the smooth conversationalists they are, they usually can cover up their inner insecurity. When they lose their emotional balance, they become extremely vulnerable, tend towards self-doubt and depressions, complain about anything and everything and unnerve those around them with their uncalculable mood shifts. Contrary to their natural disposition they may even become loud and aggressive and turn to unfair means in those situations.

Pumas need their own territory which they carefully protect from encroachment by strangers. They find it difficult to approach others in order to form a relationship. In a close relationship they are very considerate, but need a lot of attention and understanding. One has to be considerate of their vulnerability and has to try to help them get their feet back on the ground when they have escaped into their spiritual realm.

Relationships

Being a puma, you belong to the clan of frogs whose element is water. The woodpeckers (Cancer) and snakes (Scorpio) belong to the same clan. You usually get along very well with representatives of those two signs of the zodiac, since you have many basic qualities in common. In a close relationship, however, irritations can occur because of those very same shared characteristics. Only if you open up more and are in balance with your feelings, can such a relationship survive.

You and members of the turtle-clan, whose element is soil, complement each other best. Water keeps soil from drying out, and without soil as a solid foundation water cannot flow. That symbolic correlation illustrates the fact the members of both clans benefit from such a connexion. The members of the frog-clan contribute the mobility of their own element to the stable energy of the turtle-clan representatives: a mighty impulse that protects from being frozen in the dark depths of the emotional world. Vice versa the representatives of the turtle-clan offer to the members of the frog-clan stability and a secure foundation, so that their emotions don't circle aimlessly, help them realise ideas and find their inner balance which is so important to them. In practical life and on the emotional level their relationship is enjoyable, stable and rewarding to both. The human beavers (Taurus), brown-bears (Virgo) and snowgeese (Capricorn) are part of the turtle-clan.

Members of the thunderbird-clan, whose element is fire, are the opposites. Fire and water do not get along and destroy each other. In a committed relationship there can be great difficulties initially, since the representatives of the two clans instinctively feel mutually threatened, but the very contrast can be advantageous to both, since the dynamics of fire, which can be threatening at times, may be softened and the cool reserve of water on the other hand may warm up and become livelier. If the member of the thunderbird-clan shows patience and yielding and the member of the frog-clan tries to open up and become more balanced, a connexion between representatives of those clans can be very helpful for both. Red-hawks (Aries), sturgeons (Leo) and *Wapitis* (Sagittarius) belong to the clan of thunderbirds.

The element of the butterfly-clan is the air. Air, just like water, is constantly moving; in that aspect the two elements are similar. The representatives of the frog-clan and the butterfly-clan are as similar in many of their characteristics, which also means, however, that each sees a lot of his or her own faults reflected in the other one. That can cause irritations and difficulties to adjust in a committed relationship. Both should first endeavour to coordinate their mobility in the same direction and to concentrate on common goals. Members of the frog-clan can exert a stabilising effect on representatives of the clan of butterflies, because their energy usually flows in a constant stream instead of energy bursts; they act with greater caution and show more understanding, patience and constancy. The human stags (Gemini), ravens (Libra) and otters (Aquarius) belong to the clan of butterflies.

My Celtic (Tree) Horoscope

Not signs of the zodiac or animals, but trees represent the symbols of Celtic astrology. Their system is based on the two holy numbers of the Celts, namely three and seven: twenty-one trees divide the course of the year.

19 February to 29 February
Your tree is the *pine-tree*. It symbolises courage and self-assurance, resistance and organisational talent, frankness and passion, but also vanity and selective fastidiousness. The pine-tree has a high opinion of itself and likes to show off. For you personally that means you are relatively stable and able to cope with almost any situation in life. Usually you are careful and courageous. Those are ambiguous terms, but then you are ambiguous yourself. For you there is a difference between job and personal life, between friendship and love. Professionally you are willing to adapt, diligent and resilient, but personally you are rather insecure, unstable and act prematurely.

As a colleague and friend you are popular and an interesting and amusing partner, but in love matters you frequently are too demanding, give up too early and take offence easily. Your passion ignites quickly, but it often turns into disappointment. Therefore it can take a long time before you find the fulfilment of your dreams, while you generally find success and recognition quicker in your career and social life.

1 March to 10 March
Your tree is the *weeping willow*. It symbolises beauty and empathy, righteousness and honesty, but also insecurity, a susceptibility to being influenced and moodiness. Its grace and reserve grant the affection and acknowledgement of its environment. For you personally that means you are introverted, emotional and often a dreamer, but also inconsistent and moody due to inner unrest and insecurity. You often feel misunderstood and not fully appreciated.

You are sincere, do not shun difficulties and try to do justice to your environment and the demands of daily life. You appreciate arts, beauty and harmony and often have a talent for arts or music yourself. You can feel great empathy with others and sincerely share their concerns and grievances. In a close relationship you are a loving and tender partner with a lot of understanding, but you also seriously challenge your partner since you are easily hurt, frequently escape into your dream world, strongly depend on moods, have a tendency towards melancholy and let yourself be negatively influenced by others too often.

11 March to 20 March
Your tree is the *lime-tree*. It symbolises calmness and constancy, gentleness and acquiescence, but also jealousy, laziness and shifting goals. Effort, struggle and unrest are its enemies that can wear out and seriously harm it. For you personally that means you are emotional, gentle, a dreamer, have empathy and the willingness to sacrifice. You often lack determination and energy. You frequently dream of pleasant goals that are out of your reach and quarrel with your fate when your dreams don't come true. Though you are gifted in many ways, you lack persistence and goal-directed perseverance, so that a lot of things you commence get stuck in the initial phase and are not carried through. You avoid difficulties whenever possible; often you have a strong tendency towards convenience and comfort. In close relationships you often do not find the happiness you dream of in spite of your strong emotions and willingness to acquiesce, and in addition to that you frequently burden your relationship with excessive jealousy. Socially and professionally your distant friendliness earns you the sympathy and benevolence of others.

World Age, Annual Ruling Planet and Associated Symbols

As a result of the gyroscopic movement of the earth's axis (Precession) the vernal equinox, i.e. the point on the celestial sphere at which the celestial equator intersects the ecliptic, enters (anticlockwise) a different constellation around every 2100 years. The vernal equinox was at the apex of the constellation Aries around 4000 years ago. It then entered the constellation Pieces and it is currently approaching Aquarius. The constellations should not be confused with the signs of the zodiac of the same name. The latter are sections with an astrological referential framework which is directed to the vernal equinox and are not affected by the changes in the position of this point.

The time it takes for one complete revolution of the earth's axis (approximately 25,000 years) is known as a 'platonic year'. This is subdivided into twelve 'World Months' (also known as 'World Ages') each of around 2100 years, which, according to ancient astrological tradition, are defined by the effective qualities of the sign of the zodiac in which the vernal equinox is to be found at any given time. It has also been said that the sign opposite to the one in which the vernal equinox is situated exerts an additional defining force and so therefore there are two influencial polar signs.

Today we are on the threshold of the Age of Aquarius, which is distinguished by the sign of the zodiac of the same name and this sign's assigned planet, namely Uranus. Both symbolise radical changes, a heightened closeness with the universe, but also an intensification of the relationships within mankind. That the breathtaking developments in science and technology (atomic power, computers, space travel) have given rise to fundamental changes is obvious. Advancements in telecommunications and travel have turned the world into a global village and have brought people from all continents closer than they have ever been before. It is, however, too soon to tell where these developments will lead and whether they will turn out to be a blessing or a curse for mankind.

We are currently in the *Age of Pisces* and have been since around the birth of Christ. The most significant event in this period of world history was the emergence and evolvement of Christianity, an early symbol of which was the fish. The influence of the polar sign Virgo is apparent in the fundamentals of the Christian faith (humility, loving your neighbour, etc.), but also in the adoration of the Virgin Mary.

The two millennia before the birth of Christ, the *Age of Aries*, were influenced by Mars. It was a time when great battles led to the destruction of powerful empires and saw Alexander the Great lead his Greek army as far as India. The polar influence of Libra made itself apparent in the exquisite works of art of this period. The ram also played an important role in several oriental religions.

The third and fourth millennia before Christ were the *Age of Taurus*. A matter-of-fact sense of beauty and practical thought were revealed in the culture of ancient Egypt. The bull played an important role in cults throughout the whole of the Mediterranean, the most striking example of which we know about was on the island of Crete. The polar influence of Scorpio can be seen among others in the cults of death exhibited by the advanced civilisations of that time.

The *Age of Gemini* (around 6000 – 4000 BC) was characterised by a heightened intellectual and physical mobility. Notable events in this period were the propagation of writing, the foundation of the first libraries (China, Mesopotamia, Egypt) and the invention of the wheel.

We have known about *Annual Ruling Planets* for thousands of years. They were first used in south-west Asia as guides for the calculation of time – their year began in spring, so each planet therefore 'ruled' from 21 March to the following 20 March. It was not until later that the planets were believed to be of astrological importance and were henceforth incorporated into the readings of individual horoscopes and used to aid weather forecasting.

Modern astrology no longer uses the annual ruling planets, but for those who are interested, the following two charts go into the topic in a little more depth.

The Annual Ruling Planets for the Twentieth Century

Mercury
1900 1907 1914 1921 1928 1935 1942 1949 1956 1963
1970 1977 1984 1991 1998 2005 2012 2019 2026 2033

Moon
1901 1908 1915 1922 1929 1936 1943 1950 1957 1964
1971 1978 1985 1992 1999 2006 2013 2020 2027 2034

Saturn
1902 1909 1916 1923 1930 1937 1944 1951 1958 1965
1972 1979 1986 1993 2000 2007 2014 2021 2028 2035

Jupiter
1903 1910 1917 1924 1931 1938 1945 1952 1959 1966
1973 1980 1987 1994 2001 2008 2015 2022 2029 2036

Mars
1904 1911 1918 1925 1932 1939 1946 1953 1960 1967
1974 1981 1988 1995 2002 2009 2016 2023 2030 2037

Sun
1905 1912 1919 1926 1933 1940 1947 1954 1961 1968
1975 1982 1989 1996 2003 2010 2017 2024 2031 2038

Venus
1906 1913 1920 1927 1934 1941 1948 1955 1962 1969
1976 1983 1990 1997 2004 2011 2018 2025 2032 2039

'Man advances past the terrestrial sky into new universes.'
Carving from around 1530.

It was said that the ruling planet also exerted an influence on the individual constellations of the birth horoscopes and therewith exercised the following additional defining forces on those born under the respective planet:

Mercury: varied interests, critical, tendency to be rational, ambitious, eloquent, and a keen traveller.

Moon: moody, protean destiny, experiences changes in mid-life, yet succeeds in older age.

Saturn: considered, concentrated, perseveres, obstinate and reserved, slow starter but succeeds in the end.

Jupiter: generous, happy with life, optimistic, good chances of promotion.

Mars: dynamic, energetic, passionate, strong sense of self-assertion, but can also act rashly.

Sun: independent, generous, but also egocentric, self-willed and compulsive.

Venus: enthusiastic, creative, varied interests, happy with life, often only succeeds in the latter half of life.

It should be noted that the influence of the annual ruling planet is not from 1 January to 31 December, but from 21 March to 20 March of the following year.

We cannot go into details here as to the numerous associated symbols of the signs of the zodiac and the planets. However, they have been summarised below in the following order:

Sign of the Zodiac – Ruling Planet – Colours – Metal – Precious Stones – Numbers – Day of the Week

Aries: Mars – Red, Cadmium Yellow – Iron – Ruby, Jasper, Garnet, Diamond, Amethyst – Nine – Tuesday.

Taurus: Venus – Yellow, Pastel Blue, Light Green – Copper – Agate, Emerald, Sapphire, Lapis Lazuli, Turquoise, Carnelian – Five and Six – Friday.

Gemini: Mercury – Violet, Saffron Yellow – Quicksilver – Topaz, Rock Crystal, Aquamarine, Gold Beryl – Five – Wednesday.

Cancer: Moon – Green, Silver, White – Silver – Crystal, Emerald, Opal, Moonstone, Pearls – Two and Seven – Monday.

Leo: Sun – Orange, Gold, Yellow – Gold – Ruby, Diamond, Hyazinth, Gold Topaz, Catseye – One and Four – Sunday.

Virgo: Mercury – Violet, Light Blue, White – Quicksilver – Jasper, Agate, Carnelian, Topaz, Tourmaline – Five – Wednesday.

Libra: Venus – Yellow, Pink, Pastel Shades – Copper – Diamond, Beryl, Lapis Lazuli, Turquoise, Coral, Pearls – Five and Six – Friday.

Scorpio: Mars – Red, Brown, Black – Iron – Topaz, Malachite, Jasper, Ruby, Sardonyx – Nine – Tuesday.

Sagittarius: Jupiter – Blue, Purple, Warm Browns – Pewter – Dark Blue Sapphire, Turquoise, Amethyst, Lapis Lazuli, Garnet – Three – Thursday.

Capricorn: Saturn – Indigo, Dark Green, Brown, Black – Lead – Onyx, Jet, Chalcedony, Carnelian, Chrysoprase, Black Pearls – Eight and Fifteen – Saturday.

Aquarius: Uranus (previously Saturn) – Indigo, Lilac, Violet, Iridescent Colours – Lead, Aluminium, Radium – Sapphire, Amethyst, Amber, Aquamarine, Chalcedony – Eight and Fifteen – Saturday.

Pisces: Neptune (previously Jupiter) – Blue, Violet, White, Shimmering Colours – Platinum, Pewter – Chrysolite, Sapphire, Topaz, Opal, Mother of Pearl, Crystal – Three – Thursday.

III.
How to Work Out Your Ascendant

Since the Greenwich Meridian runs longitudinally through Great Britain, the time on your birth certificate equals world time. In order to be able to read off your ascendant from the table on the relevant page referring to the day of your birth (p. 84ff.) you have to transform your time of birth, which is quoted in world time, into local time. If you do not know your exact time of birth, you can find it out by enquiring at the registry office in the town in which you were born. If you were born at a time when summer time applied, your time of birth in world time is equal to your actual time of birth minus one hour.

The local time depends on the longitude of your place of birth. For each degree of longitude to the east of the Greenwich Meridian you must add on four minutes to your time of birth according to world time; for each degree west you must deduct four minutes. In order to avoid you having to carry out lengthy research, we have compiled a regional chart for Great Britain and Northern Ireland on the page opposite. The chart lists major towns and cities and the number of minutes you need to add (e.g., +12) or subtract (e.g., -8). If your place of birth is not listed, look on a map and roughly locate another town which is included in the list and which is on the same longitude as your place of birth and add or subtract the requisite number of minutes listed to or from your time of birth in world time.

Regional Chart to Determine Your Ascendant

PLACE	Min.	PLACE	Min.	PLACE	Min.
Aberdeen	-8	Gateshead	-6	Newry	-25
Armagh	-27	Glasgow	-17	Northampton	-3
Ayr	-18	Gloucester	-9	Norwich	+6
Bath	-9	Greenock	-19	Nottingham	-4
Belfast	-24	Grimsby	0	Oxford	-5
Birkenhead	-12	Halifax	-7	Paisley	-14
Birmingham	-7	Harrogate	-6	Perth	-14
Blackpool	-12	Hastings	+3	Peterborough	-1
Boston	0	Huddersfield	-7	Plymouth	-16
Bournemouth	-8	Inverness	-17	Poole	-8
Bradford	-7	Ipswich	+5	Portsmouth	-4
Brighton	0	Kilmarnock	-18	Preston	-11
Bristol	-10	Kingston upon		Reading	-4
Cambridge	+1	Hull	-1	Rhondda	-14
Cardiff	-13	Kirkcaldy	-13	Rotherham	-6
Carlisle	-12	Lancaster	-11	Rugby	-5
Chester	-12	Leeds	-6	Sheffield	-6
Chesterfield	-6	Leicester	-4	South Shields	-6
Coatbridge	-16	Lincoln	-2	Southampton	-5
Colchester	+4	Liverpool	-12	Southend	+3
Coventry	-6	London	+1	Stafford	-9
Darlington	-6	Londonderry	-30	Stockport	-8
Derby	-6	Luton	-2	Stockton on Tees	-6
Dover	+5	Maidstone	+2	Stoke on Trent	-8
Dudley	-8	Manchester	-7	Sunderland	-6
Dumfries	-14	Margate	+6	Swansea	-16
Dundee	-12	Middlesbrough	-5	Torbay	-14
Eastbourne	+1	Motherwell a.	-16	Tynemouth	-6
Edinburgh	-13	Newcastle		Whitehaven	-14
Enniskillen	-30	upon Tyne	-6	Worcester	-7
Exeter	-14	Newport	-12	York	-4

Your Ascendant on 19 February

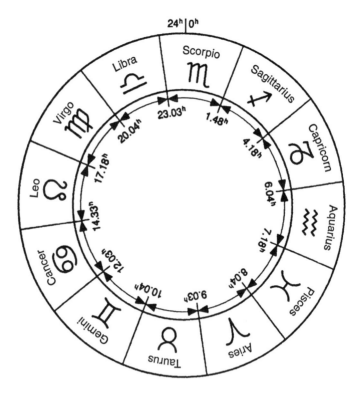

Your Ascendant on 20 February

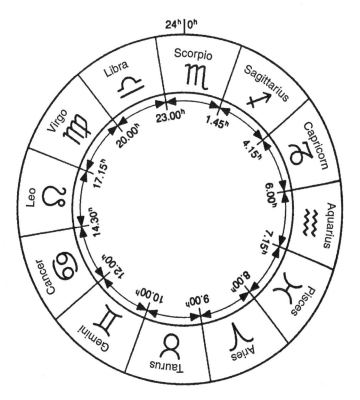

Your Ascendant on 21 February

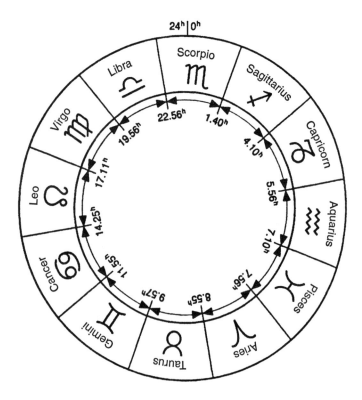

Your Ascendant on 22 February

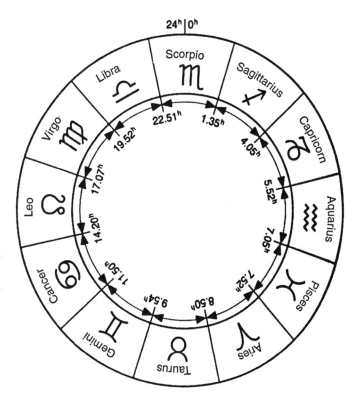

Your Ascendant on 23 February

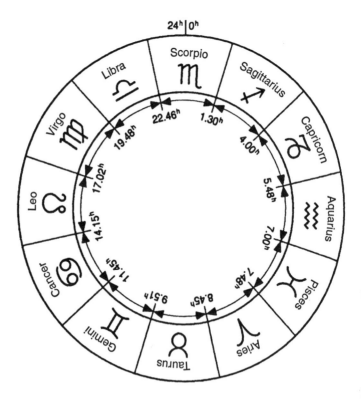

Your Ascendant on 24 February

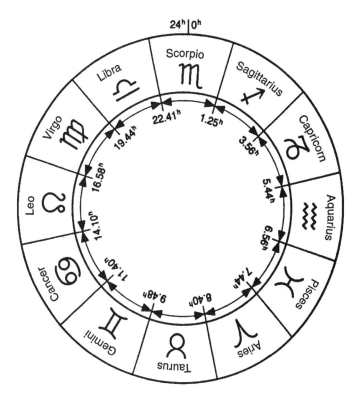

Your Ascendant on 25 February

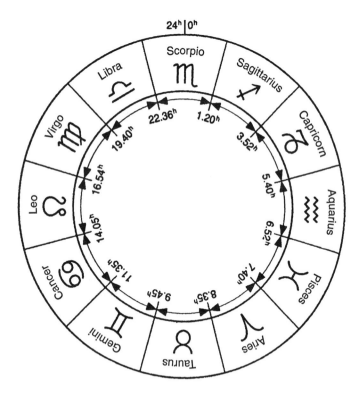

Your Ascendant on 26 February

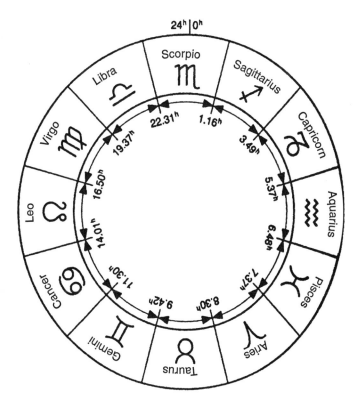

Your Ascendant on 27 February

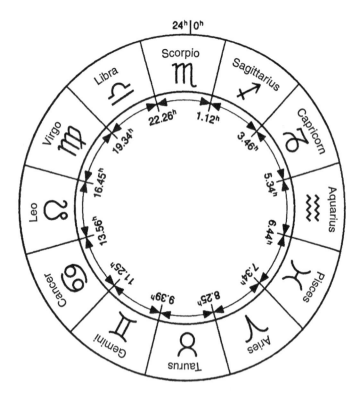

Your Ascendant on 28 February

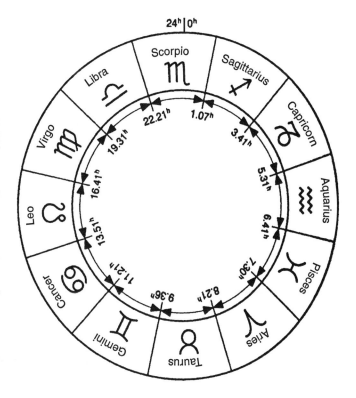

Your Ascendant on 29 February

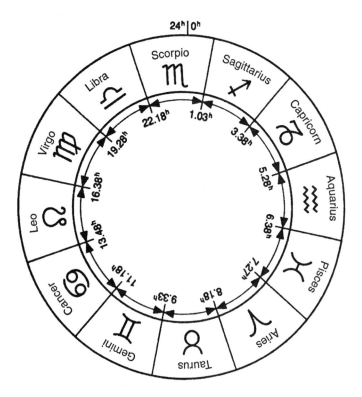

Your Ascendant on 1 March

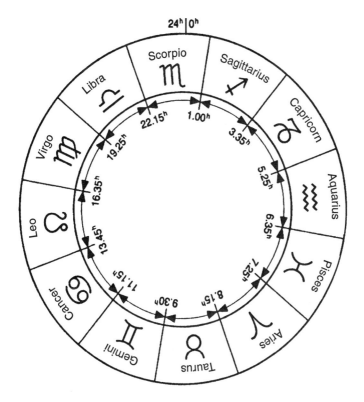

Your Ascendant on 2 March

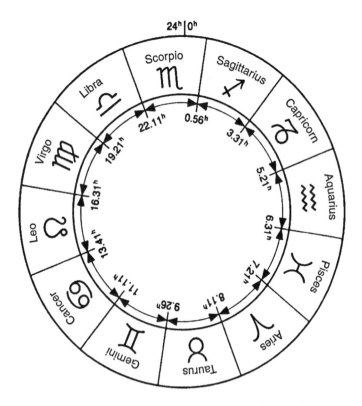

Your Ascendant on 3 March

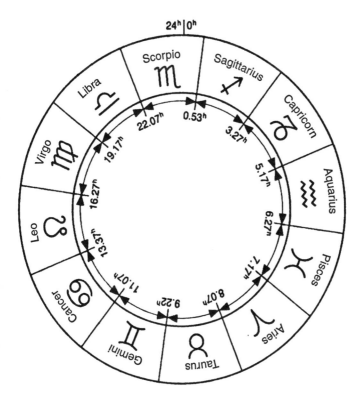

Your Ascendant on 4 March

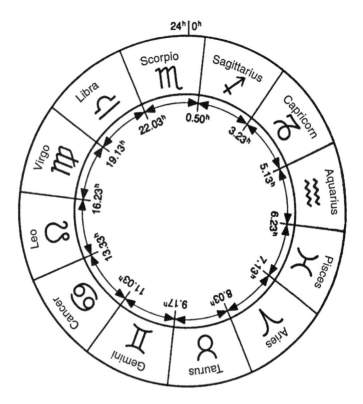

Your Ascendant on 5 March

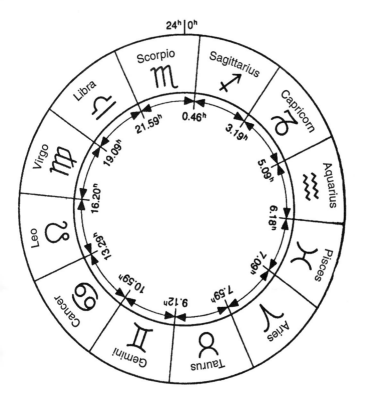

Your Ascendant on 6 March

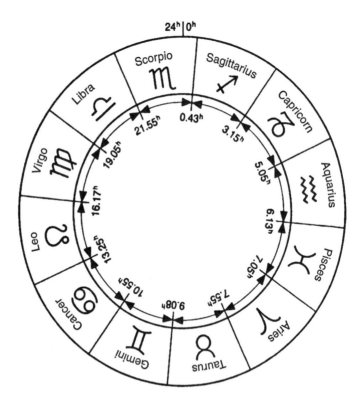

Your Ascendant on 7 March

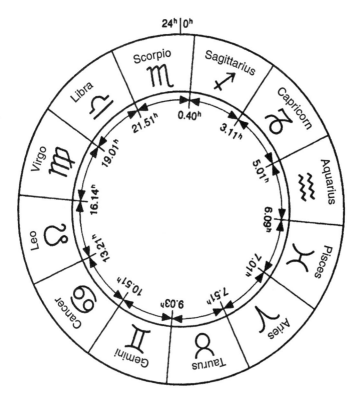

Your Ascendant on 8 March

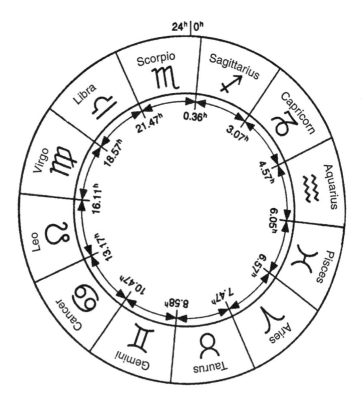

Your Ascendant on 9 March

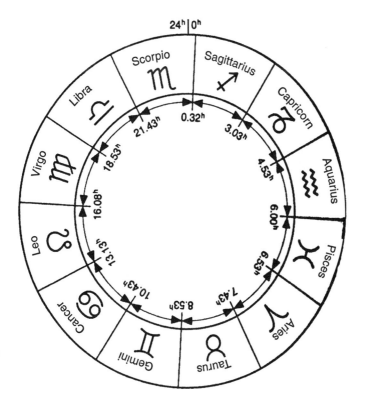

Your Ascendant on 10 March

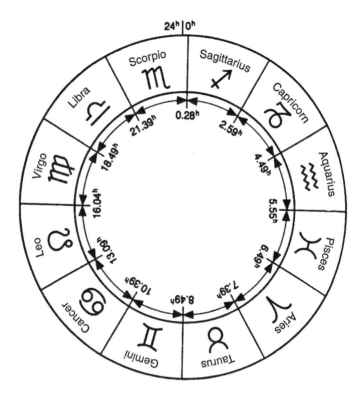

Your Ascendant on 11 March

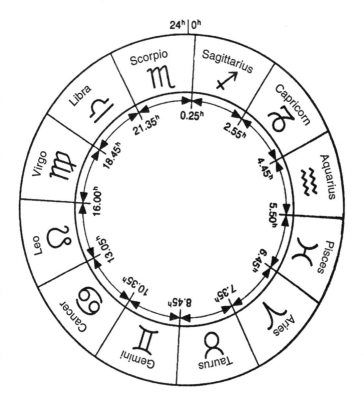

Your Ascendant on 12 March

Your Ascendant on 13 March

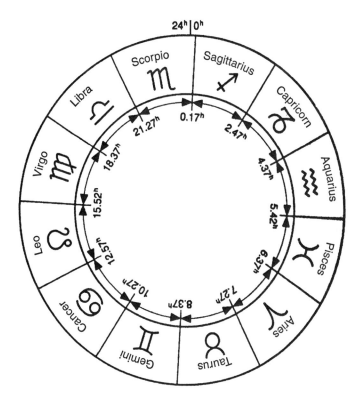

Your Ascendant on 14 March

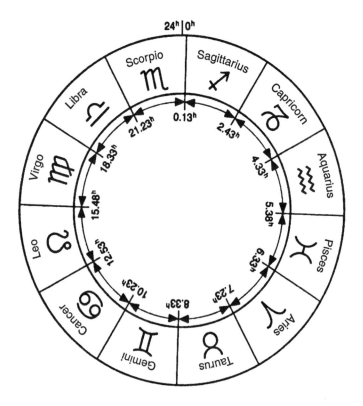

Your Ascendant on 15 March

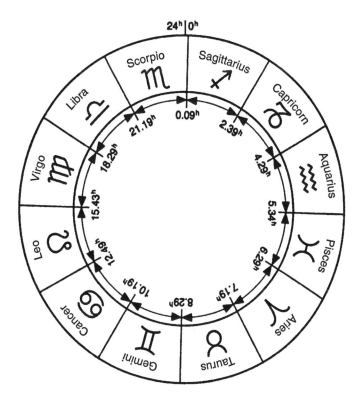

Your Ascendant on 16 March

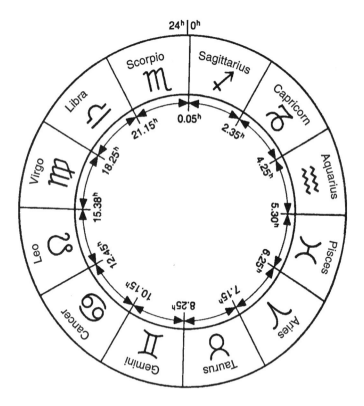

Your Ascendant on 17 March

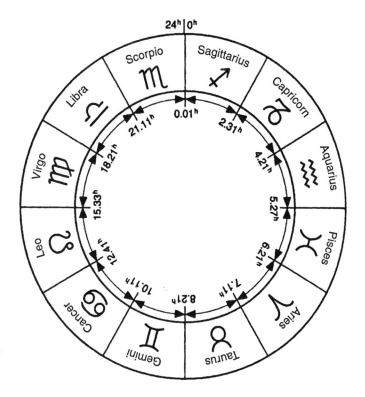

Your Ascendant on 18 March

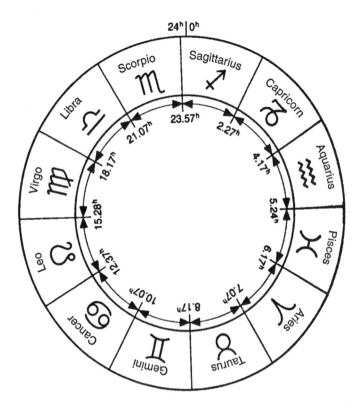

Your Ascendant on 19 March

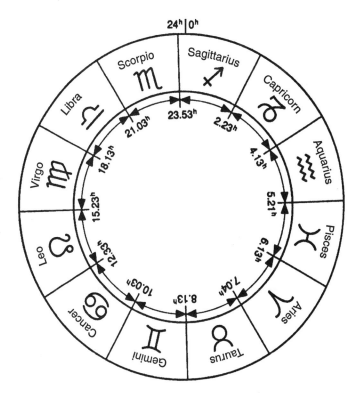

Your Ascendant on 20 March

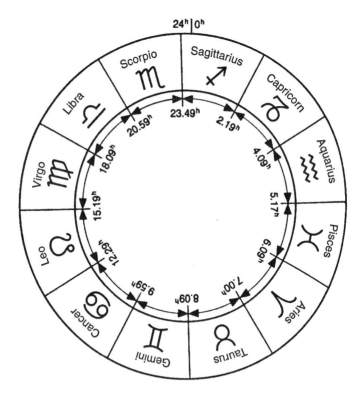

IV.
Who, What, Where, When

Famous Pisceans

19 February
Nikolaus Kopernikus, German astronomer (1473-1543)
Luigi Boccherini, Italian composer and cellist (1743-1805)
Sven Hedin, Swedish scientist (1865-1952)
André Breton, French writer (1896-1966)
Andrew, The Duke of York (1960)

20 February
Enzo Ferrari, Italian race car constructor (1898-1988)
Sidney Poitier, American actor (1924)
Robert Altmann, American film director (1925)
Kurt Cobain, American rock musician (1967-1993)

21 February
Sasha Guitry, French writer (1885-1957)
Raymond Queneau, French writer (1903-1976)
Alexej N. Kossygin, Soviet politician (1904-1980)
Wystan Hugh Auden, English writer (1907-1973)

22 February
George Washington,
American general and politician (1732-1799)
Arthur Schopenhauer, German philosopher (1788-1860)
Luis Bunuel, Spanish film director (1900-1983)
Niki Lauda, Austrian race car driver (1949)

23 February
Georg Friedrich Händel, German composer (1685-1759)
Meyer Amschel Rothschild, German banker (1743-1812)
Kasimir Malevitch, Russian painter (1878-1935)
Erich Kästner, German writer (1899-1974)

24 February
Karl V., German emperor (1500-1558)
Charles Le Brun, French painter (1619-1690)
George Moore, Anglo-Irish writer (1852-1933)
Ulrich de Maizière, German general (1912)
Alain Prost, French race car driver (1955)

25 February
Pierre Auguste Renoir, French painter (1841-1919)
Karl May, German writer (1842-1912)
Benedetto Croce, Italian philosopher (1866-1952)
Anthony Burgess, British actor (1917)

26 February
Victor Hugo, French writer (1802-1885)
Buffalo Bill, American pioneer (1846-1917)
Giulio Natta, Italian chemist (1903-1979)
Antoine 'Fats' Domino, American Rock musician (1928)
Johnny Cash, American singer (1932)

27 February
Enrico Caruso, Italian singer (1873-1921)
John Steinbeck, American writer (1902-1968)
James Thomas Farrell, American writer (1904-1979)
Elizabeth Taylor, British-American actress (1932)

28 February
Michel Eyquem de Montaigne,
French philosopher (1533-1592)
Marcel Pagnol, French playwright (1895-1974)
Linus Carl Pauling, American chemist (1901-1994)

29 February
Pope Paul III (1468-1549)
Gioachino Rossini, Italian composer (1792-1868)
Michèle Morgan, French actress (1920)

1 March
Frédéric Chopin, Polish composer and pianist (1810-1849)
Théophile Delcassé, French politician (1852-1923)
Oskar Kokoschka, Austrian painter and poet (1886-1980)
Glenn Miller, American jazz musician (1904-1944)
Yitzhak Rabin, Israelite politician (1922-1995)
Harry Belafonte, American singer (1927)

2 March
Friedrich Smetana, Czech composer (1824-1884)
Pope Pius XXII (1876-1950)
Kurt Weill, German composer (1900-1950)
Michail Gorbachev, Soviet politician (1931)
John Irving, American writer (1942)

3 March
William Godwin, British writer (1756-1836)
Arthur Kornberg, American biochemist (1918)
Ion Illiescu, Rumanian politician (1930)
Ariane Mnouchkine, French actress and film director (1939)

4 March
Henry the Sailor, Portuguese infante (1394-1460)
Antonio Vivaldi, Italian composer (1678-1741)
Henry Raeburn, Scottish painter (1756-1823)
Alan Sillitoe, British writer (1928)
Jim Clark, Scottish race car driver (1936-1968)

5 March
Henry II, King of England (1133-1189)
Rosa Luxemburg, German politician (1870-1919)
Reginald 'Rex' Harrison, British actor (1908-1990)
James Tobin, American national economist (1918)

6 March
Michelangelo, Italian sculptor and painter (1475-1564)
Jakob Fugger, German trader and banker (1459-1525)
Savinien de Cyrano de Bergerac, French writer (1619-1655)
Stanislav Jerzytec, Polish poet and satirist (1909-1966)
Gabriel Garcia Márquez, Columbian writer (1928)

7 March
Maurice Ravel, French composer (1875-1937)
Heinz Rühmann, German actor (1902-1994)
Jacques Chaban-Delmas, French politician (1914)
Ivan Lendl, American tennis player (1960)

8 March
Philipp Emanuel Bach, German composer (1714-1788)
Edward Kendall, American biochemist (1886-1972)
Otto Hahn, German chemist (1879-1968)
Shrimati Uma Nehru, Indian politician (1884-1968)

9 March
Amerigo Vespucci, Italian navigator (1451-1512)
Jean Baptiste Kléber, French general (1753-1800)
Rex Warner, English writer and philologist (1905)
Juri Gagarin, Soviet cosmonaut (1934-1968)

10 March

Lorenzo da Ponte, Italian librettist (1749-1838)
Luise, Queen of Prussia (1776-1810)
Joseph von Eichendorff, German writer (1788-1857)
Boris Vian, French writer (1920-1959)
Edward, Earl of Wessex (1964)

11 March

Urbain Jean Joseph Leverrier, French astronomer (1811-1877)
Marius Petipa, French dancer (1818-1910)
Sir Harold Wilson, British politician (1916-1995)

12 March

Robert Kirchhoff, German physicist (1824-1887)
Kemal Atatürk, Turkish officer and politician (1881-1938)
Alberto Burri, Italian material sculptor (1914-1995)
Liza Minelli, American actress and singer (1946)

13 March

Joseph II, Emperor of the Roman Empire (1741-1790)
Karl Friedrich Schinkel, German architect (1781-1841)
Franz Roubaud, Russian painter (1856-1928)
Ron L. Hubbard, American founder of sect (1911-1986)

14 March

Johann Strauss, Austrian composer (1804-1849)
Albert Einstein, German physicist (1879-1955)
André Pieyre de Mandiargues, French writer (1909)
Michael Caine, British actor (1933)
Albert, Hereditary Prince of Monaco (1958)

15 March
Andrew Jackson, the 7th President of the U.S.A (1767-1845)
Earl von Stauffenberg, German resistance fighter (1905-1944)
Zarah Leander, Swedish actress (1907-1981)

16 March
Antoine-Jean Gros, French painter (1771-1835)
Georg Simon Ohm, German physicist (1789-1854)
Jerry Lewis, American film comedian (1926)
Bernardo Bertolucci, Italian film director (1940)

17 March
Gottlieb Daimler, German engineer (1834-1900)
Nat 'King' Cole, American jazz musician (1917-1965)
Rudolf Nurejew, Austrian dancer (1838-1993)

18 March
Marie-Madeleine Countess de Lafayette,
French writer (1634-1693)
Rudolf Diesel, German engineer and inventor (1858-1913)
Arthur Neville Chamberlain, British politician (1869-1940)
Tatjana Gsovsky, German-Russian dancer (1901-1993)
John Updike, American writer (1932)

19 March
David Livingstone, English Africa researcher (1813-1873)
Frédéric Joliot-Curie, French Physicist (1900-1958)
Elder James Olson, American lyric poet (1909)

20 March
Franz Napoléon Bonaparte, Duke of Reichstadt (1811-1832)
Henrik Ibsen, Norwegian poet and writer (1828-1906)
Vera Fyodorovna, Russian writer (1905-1973)
Ralph Giordano, German writer and journalist (1923)

Important Historical Events

19 February

1855	The first international weather chart is created with the help of a telegraph.
1861	Chattel slavery is abolished in Russia and many farmers can thus be liberated.
1986	The Russian space shuttle 'Mir' is sent on its orbit around the earth.

20 February

1810	The Tyrolese freedom fighter Andreas Hofer is shot dead by French soldiers.
1827	World premiere of the overture on William Shakespeare's 'A Midnight Summer Dream' by Felix Mendelssohn Bartholdy
1952	The American actor Humphrey Bogart receives his only Oscar for his performance in the film 'African Queen'.

21 February

1795	The Scotsman Mungo Park starts off on the first research expedition of Central Africa.
1916	The German attack on Verdun triggers the greatest battle of World War I.
1965	The nationalistic black leader Malcolm X is shot dead during his speech in Harlem, New York. He actively supported forceful resistance against white America.

22 February

1371	Robert Stuart becomes King of Scotland and thus founds the House of Stuart.
1808	Upon the entering of Russian troops into Finland Sweden is forced to give up Finland to Russia.
1819	The U.S. receive Florida from Spain.

23 February

1766   After the death of the former King of Poland, the Duke of Lorraine and Bar, the Duchy of Lorraine becomes the property of France.

24 February

1525   In the battle for Italy Emperor Charles V defeats the French King Francois I at Pavia.

1848   The Communist Manifestation by Karl Marx and Friedrich Engels is first published.

1848   The 'Civilian King', Louis Philippe, abdicates and the Republic of France is proclaimed.

25 February

1516   The Dutch Scholar Erasmus of Rotterdam finishes his translation of the Bible from Greek.

1986   In an unbloody revolt on the Philippines the Dictator Ferdinand Marcos is overthrown.

1994   In Hebron a militant Jewish settler shoots 29 Palestinians dead.

26 February

1839   The most difficult obstacle race, the Grand National Steeplechase in Aintree near Liverpool, takes place for the first time.

1871   In the preliminary Peace of Versailles France must give up the Alsace and Lorraine to Germany.

1993   A bomb deposited by Islamic terrorists explodes at the World Trade Center in New York.

27 February

1594   The first Bourbon is enthroned as French King Henry IV at the Cathedral of Chartres.

1973   200 Indians occupy Wounded Knee in South Dakota to publicly claim their rights.

1974   The Swedish Parliament concludes a new constitution that changes the country into a parliamentary monarchy.

28 February

1974	After Prime Minister Edward Heath resigns from Office, Labour Chief Harold Wilson becomes the leader of a minority government.
1976	Spain gives up the western Sahara to Morocco and Mauritania.
1986	The Swedish Prime Minister Olof Palme is assassinated in the streets of Stockholm.
1991	Saddam Hussein, Head of State of Iraq, capitulates in the Gulf War.

29 February

1920	The Provisional National Assembly of Czechoslovakia concludes a constitution based on the French model.
1940	Great Britain restricts the new purchases of land by Jewish settlers in Palestine.
1960	The Moroccan port city of Agadir is destroyed by a severe earthquake, which kills about 10,000 people.

1 March

1565	Foundation of the Brazilian metropolis Rio de Janeiro.
1815	Napoleon returns from his exile on the Mediterranean Isle of Elba to recapture his empire. He reigns for 100 days.
1903	The police have found a new investigative method by examining fingerprints.

2 March

1724	Georg Friedrich Händel's opera 'Julius Caesar in Egypt' celebrates its premiere and is very successful.
1923	The Austrian author Felix Salter creates the figure of the fawn 'Bambi'.
1939	In his inaugural journey Pope Pius XII makes his appeal for peace and tries to mediate in vain in World War II.

3 March

1875   World premiere of the opera 'Carmen' by Georges Bizet

1924   After ruling for 600 years the Osmanian Caliphate is deposed by the Turkish National Assembly.

1960   Bishop Laurean Rugambwa, appointed by Pope John XIII, becomes the first black cardinal.

4 March

1801   Thomas Jefferson becomes the third president of the U.S.A. in Washington.

1928   British Sir Frederick Leigh of Kandahar donates the first cup for a ski race, thus making Alpine skiing an official sport.

1947   In Dunkirk France and Great Britain sign a military mutual assistance pact with the objective to protect themselves from Germany.

5 March

1922   The film 'Nosferatu - A Symphony of Horror', based on the source by Bram Stoker, is shown in the cinemas.

1979   Planet Jupiter and its moons are passed by the U.S. space probe 'Voyager' for the very first time.

6 March

1714   The Roman-German Emperor Charles VI denounces his succession to the throne in Spain and therewith ends the hereditary war with France.

1968   Blast-off for the construction of the Euphrates dike in Tabaka/Syria creating the Assad Reservoir.

1992   The computer virus Michelangelo appears.

7 March

1914	Publishing of the novel 'Dubliners' by James Joyce.
1920	Syrian freedom fighters proclaim the independence of their country which, however, is occupied by France one year later.
1945	U.S. troops capture the bridge of Remagen, thus enabling the quick advance of the Allies.

8 March

1941	After public protests martial law is established in Northern Holland.
1963	After a military coup the socialist Bath-party gains power in Syria.
1971	Joe Frazier defeats Muhammad Ali.

9 March

1796	Wedding between Napoleon Bonaparte and Joséphine de Beauharnais.
1842	Giuseppe Verdi achieves fame with his opera 'Nabucco'.
1932	Eamon de Valera becomes Irish Prime Minister.

10 March

1661	French King Louis XIV takes over the reign and becomes the model of absolutism.
1952	In Cuba General Fulgenico Batista takes over power with the help of the army.
1969	The murderer of the American civil rights activist Martin Luther King is sentenced to 99 years in prison.

11 March

1812	Prussian King William III grants equal rights to Jewish citizens.
1972	World premiere of the film 'The Godfather' by Francis Ford Coppola
1990	Lithuania breaks away from the Soviet Union with a one-sided declaration of independence.

12 March

1930	The Indian freedom fighter Mahatma Gandhi starts on his so-called 'salt march' with the objective to boycott the salt monopoly of the British colonial government.
1933	Successful production of polyethylene, synthetic foil, in London
1947	Harry Truman proclaims his doctrine, according to which the U.S. declares to support all non-Communist countries.

13 March

1938	One day after German troops enter Austria, Adolf Hitler declares the 'Anschluß' of Austria to the German Reich.
1991	Former Prime Minister and Chief of Party of the GDR, Erich Honecker, flees to Moscow.

14 March

1937	Pope Pius XI sharply criticises the nazi terror against the Church.
1953	Nikita Chrushev becomes head of the Communist Party after Stalin's death.
1989	Zita, last Empress of Austria and Queen of Hungary, passes away at the age of 96.
1993	Andorra becomes democratic; parties and unions are now authorized.

15 March

44 AC	Gaius Julius Caesar is assassinated by members of the Senate, among them Brutus, his own son.
1901	Paintings by Vincent van Gogh are exhibited in Paris.
1922	The Egyptian public revolts under Sultan Ahmad Fuad and gains independence.
1951	The Iranian government orders the nationalisation of the country's crude oil industry.
1991	The French-Canadian ice skating team Isabelle and Paul Duchesnay wins the gold medal at the World Ice Skating Championship in Munich.

16 March

1521	The Portuguese circumnavigator Magellan discovers the Philippines.
1960	Alfred Hitchcock's masterpiece 'Psycho' is shown at the cinemas.
1968	American soldiers create a massacre among the civilians of the Vietnamese village My Lai.
1986	The great majority of the Swiss public vote against Switzerland becoming a member of the U.N.

17 March

180	In Vindobona (Vienna) the Roman Emperor and Philosopher Marc Aurel succumbs to the pest.
1908	In order to assist the search for a criminal the English paper 'Daily Mirror' publishes police photos for the first time.
1929	The German Adam Opel AG is taken over by General Motors.
1992	During a public vote among the white population of South Africa 68.7 % of the people vote for the abolishment of Apartheid.

18 March

1229   The German Emperor Friedrich II crowns himself as King of Jerusalem and therewith underlines his independence from the Pope.

1891   The first telephone conversation between Paris and London is carried out.

1922   Mahatma Gandhi, the leader of the non-violent Indian liberty movement, is sentenced to six years of imprisonment by the English colonial government.

1965   The Soviet cosmonaut Alexej Leonov leaves the space ship 'Woschod II' and floats freely in space for several minutes.

19 March

1922   In memory of the Swedish King Gustav Wasa the journalist Anders Pers founds the Wasa Cross Country Skiing Race.

1945   Facing the imminent defeat, Hitler orders the destruction of all property and industrial plants in Germany but is undermined by Minister of Armament Speer.

1964   For the first time the 5.8 kilometre long tunnel through the Great St. Bernhard opens up for traffic through the Alps.

20 March

1926   General Chiang Kaishek takes over the leadership of the national party in China.

1933   SS-Leader Heinrich Himmler orders the construction of the first concentration camp near Dachau.

1956   France acknowledges the independence of Tunesia. It is the first North African property France gives up.